Lecture Notes in Computer Science 15430

The series Lecture Notes in Computer Science (LNCS), including its subseries Lecture Notes in Artificial Intelligence (LNAI) and Lecture Notes in Bioinformatics (LNBI), has established itself as a medium for the publication of new developments in computer science and information technology research, teaching, and education.

LNCS enjoys close cooperation with the computer science R & D community, the series counts many renowned academics among its volume editors and paper authors, and collaborates with prestigious societies. Its mission is to serve this international community by providing an invaluable service, mainly focused on the publication of conference and workshop proceedings and postproceedings. LNCS commenced publication in 1973.

Sheng He · Liang-Jie Zhang
Editors

Services Computing – SCC 2024

21st International Conference
Held as Part of the Services Conference Federation, SCF 2024
Bangkok, Thailand, November 16–19, 2024
Proceedings

Springer

Editors
Sheng He
Kingdee International Software Group Co., Ltd.
Shenzhen, China

Liang-Jie Zhang
Shenzhen University
Shenzhen, China

ISSN 0302-9743 ISSN 1611-3349 (electronic)
Lecture Notes in Computer Science
ISBN 978-3-031-76999-3 ISBN 978-3-031-77000-5 (eBook)
https://doi.org/10.1007/978-3-031-77000-5

This Springer imprint is published by the registered company Springer Nature Switzerland AG
The registered company address is: Gewerbestrasse 11, 6330 Cham, Switzerland

Preface

Services account for a major part of the IT industry today. Companies increasingly like to focus on their core expertise area and use IT services to address all their peripheral needs. Services computing is a new science that aims to study and better understand the foundations of this highly popular industry. It covers the science and technology of leveraging computing and information technology to model, create, operate, and manage business services.

The 2024 International Conference on Services Computing (SCC 2024) contributed to building the pillars of this important science and shaping the future of services computing. The event was a prime international forum for both researchers and industry practitioners to exchange the latest fundamental advances in the state of the art and practice of business modeling, business consulting, solution creation, service delivery, and software architecture design, development, and deployment.

This volume presents the papers accepted at SCC 2024, held in Bangkok, Thailand, during November 16 – November 19, 2024. For SCC 2024, we accepted 7 full papers. Each was single-blind reviewed and selected by at least three independent members of the Program Committee in a single-blind review process.

We are pleased to thank the authors whose submissions and participation made this conference possible. We also want to express our thanks to the Organizing Committee and Program Committee members, for their dedication in helping to organize the conference and reviewing the submissions. We owe special thanks to the on-site speakers for their impressive speeches.

September 2024

Sheng He
Liang-Jie Zhang

Organization

Program Chair

Sheng He	Kingdee International Software Group Co., Ltd., China

Services Conference Federation (SCF 2024)

General Chairs

Ali Arsanjani	Google, USA
Wu Chou	Essenlix Corporation, USA

Program Chair

Liang-Jie Zhang	Shenzhen University, China

CFO

Min Luo	Georgia Tech, USA

Operation Committee

Jing Zeng	China Gridcom Co., Ltd., China
Yishuang Ning	Tsinghua University, China
Sheng He	Kingdee International Software Group Co., Ltd., China
Zhuolin Mei	Jiujiang University, China

Steering Committee

Calton Pu (Co-chair)	Georgia Tech, USA
Liang-Jie Zhang (Co-chair)	Shenzhen University, China

SCC 2024 Program Committee

Lizhen Cui	Shandong University, China
Kenneth Fletcher	University of Massachusetts Boston, USA
Alfredo Goldman	USP, Brazil
Shigeru Hosono	Tokyo University of Technology, Japan
Xiaodong Liu	Chinese Academy of Sciences, China
Muhammad Younas	Oxford Brookes University, UK
Sanjay Chaudhary	Ahmedabad University, India
Shijun Liu	Shandong University, China
Xin Luo	Chongqing University, China
Marcio Oikawa	University of São Caetano do Sul, Brazil
Andre Luis Schwerz	Federal University of Technology Paraná, Brazil
Jun Shen	University of Wollongong, Australia
Yang Syu	National Taipei University of Education, Taiwan
Yu-Bin Yang	Nanjing University, China

Conference Sponsor – Services Society

The Services Society (S2) is a non-profit professional organization that has been created to promote worldwide research and technical collaboration in services innovations among academia and industrial professionals. Its members are volunteers from industry and academia with common interests. S2 is registered in the USA as a "501(c) organization", which means that it is an American tax-exempt nonprofit organization. S2 collaborates with other professional organizations to sponsor or co-sponsor conferences and to promote an effective services curriculum in colleges and universities. S2 initiates and promotes a "Services University" program worldwide to bridge the gap between industrial needs and university instruction.

The Services Sector accounted for 79.5% of the GDP of the USA in 2016. The Services Society has formed 5 Special Interest Groups (SIGs) to support technology and domain-specific professional activities.

- Special Interest Group on Services Computing (SIG-SC)
- Special Interest Group on Big Data (SIG-BD)
- Special Interest Group on Cloud Computing (SIG-CLOUD)
- Special Interest Group on Artificial Intelligence (SIG-AI)
- Special Interest Group on Metaverse (SIG-Metaverse)

About the Services Conference Federation (SCF)

As the founding member of the Services Conference Federation (SCF), the first **International Conference on Web Services (ICWS)** was held in June 2003 in Las Vegas, USA. Meanwhile, the First International Conference on Web Services - Europe 2003 (ICWS-Europe 2003) was held in Germany in October 2003. ICWS-Europe 2003 was an extended event of the 2003 International Conference on Web Services (ICWS 2003) in Europe. In 2004, ICWS-Europe was changed to the European Conference on Web Services (ECOWS), which was held at Erfurt, Germany. Sponsored by the Services Society and Springer, SCF 2018 and SCF 2019 were held successfully in Seattle and San Diego, USA. SCF 2020 and SCF 2021 were held successfully online and in Shenzhen, China. SCF 2022 and 2023 were held successfully in Hawaii, USA. To celebrate its 21st birthday, SCF 2024 was held on November 16 - 19, 2024, in Bangkok, Thailand.

In the past 21 years, the ICWS community has expanded from Web engineering innovations to scientific research for the whole services industry. Service delivery platforms have been expanded to mobile platforms, Internet of Things, cloud computing, and edge computing. The services ecosystem has gradually been enabled, value added, and intelligence embedded through enabling technologies such as big data, artificial intelligence, and cognitive computing. In the coming years, all transactions with multiple parties involved will be transformed to blockchain.

Based on technology trends and best practices in the field, the Services Conference Federation (SCF) will continue serving as the conference umbrella's code name for all services-related conferences. SCF 2024 defined the future of New ABCDE (AI, Blockchain, Cloud, BigData & IOT) and entered the 5G for Services Era. The theme of ICWS 2024 was Web-based Services for Metaverse Era. We are very proud to announce that SCF 2024's 10 co-located theme topic conferences all centered around "services", with each focusing on exploring different themes (web-based services, cloud-based services, Big Data-based services, services innovation lifecycle, AI-driven ubiquitous services, blockchain-driven trust service ecosystems, industry-specific services and applications, and emerging service-oriented technologies).

- Bigger Platform: The 10 collocated conferences (SCF 2024) were sponsored by the Services Society, which is the world-leading not-for-profit organization (501(c)(3)) dedicated to the service of more than 30,000 worldwide Services Computing researchers and practitioners. A bigger platform means bigger opportunities for all volunteers, authors, and participants. Meanwhile, Springer provided sponsorship of the best paper awards and other professional activities. All the 10 conference proceedings of SCF 2024 were published by Springer and indexed in the ISI Conference Proceedings Citation Index (included in Web of Science), Engineering Index EI (Compendex and Inspec databases), DBLP, Google Scholar, IO-Port, MathSciNet, Scopus, and ZBlMath.

- Brighter Future: While celebrating the 2024 version of ICWS, SCF 2024 highlighted the International Conference on Blockchain (ICBC 2024) and the International Conference on Metaverse (Metaverse 2024) to build the fundamental infrastructure for enabling secure and trusted services ecosystems and cover immersive services for all vertical industries and area solutions. It put its focus on industry-specific services for digital transformation. This will lead our community members to create their own brighter future.
- Better Model: SCF 2024 continued to leverage the invented Conference Blockchain Model (CBM) to innovate the organizing practices for all the 10 theme conferences. Senior researchers in the field are welcome to submit proposals to serve as CBM Ambassador for an individual conference to start better interactions during your leadership role in organizing future SCF conferences.

Contents

Extracting Tuple-Based Service Demands with Large Language Models for Automated Service Composition

Chih-Jung Hsu[1(✉)], Yu-Xiang Luo[2], Yi-Chen Mao[2], Chien-Min Wang[1], and Yang Syu[3]

[1] Institute of Information Science, Academia Sinica, Taipei, Taiwan
{hsu8591,cmwang}@iis.sinica.edu.tw

[2] Department of Computer Science and Information Engineering, National Taiwan University, Taipei, Taiwan
{b10902037,b10902103}@csie.ntu.edu.tw

[3] Department of Information Science, National Taipei University of Education, Taipei, Taiwan
yangsyu@mail.ntue.edu.tw

Abstract. Existing Automated Service Composition (ASC) approaches typically require inputs to be in a designated form. These, namely tuples, pose challenges due to the significant divergence from the most commonly used and straightforward formats for expressing software requirements. In our previous work, we developed a rule-based approach that necessitated substantial resources for analyzing the content of requirements and establishing appropriate rules. Given the recent successes in field research involving large language models (LLMs)-where significant achievements have been made in real-time automatic text generation tasks-we propose leveraging LLMs for ASC to extract critical tuple-based information. We have created a new dataset to simulate everyday service demands and have established clear guidelines regarding service demand types (e.g., input and output). Moreover, we have implemented an appropriate workflow that optimizes LLMs performance. Our experiments and results demonstrate that our proposed LLMs-based approach not only achieves extraordinary performance and reliability at a lower cost but also outperforms the complex rule-based solutions that were previously employed.

Keywords: Automatic Service Composition · Service Description · Large Language Model

1 Introduction

Automated Service Composition (ASC) has been a widely studied research subject in academia for many years [3,15,18]. Research on ASC [15] focuses on the complete generation of a composite service from scratch to meet user requests or customer requirements. One of the most critical issues concerning the efficient

S. He and L.-J. Zhang (Eds.): SCF/SCC 2024, LNCS 15430, pp. 1–16, 2025.
https://doi.org/10.1007/978-3-031-77000-5_1

connection between ASC and software requirements is extracting accurate information from manually created documents without a unified format. Moreover, most of these documents are written in natural language, expressing human thoughts, making it challenging to utilize this unprocessed information. As a result, our goal is to design a precise and flexible automatic model capable of transforming human-written requirement descriptions into a unified tuple-based format.

In our previous work [14,15], we provided a rule-based solution. Through the analysis of requirement descriptions, we observed specific rules related to the positioning of words. We discovered the relationship between keywords and target words using POS tags. Finally, we developed appropriate rules to extract keywords for different classifications. However, analyzing documents for rule extraction consumes considerable resources and lacks flexibility due to the need for repeating observations on different datasets. Therefore, we propose an efficient and effective approach in this paper.

We employ large language models (LLMs) to recognize requirement descriptions and extract critical partitions. In recent years, LLMs has demonstrated significant performance in text generation; by inputting relevant prompt information, users can receive beneficial responses from the model's output. We analyze the features of mainstream LLMs and adjust our design to meet our objectives. In the following section, we introduce our approaches, including dataset construction, models, prompt design, fine-tuning, and experimental for implementing the extraction of tuple-based service demands through LLMs.

With rigorous experimental results, we demonstrate that LLMs-based methods can effectively address the challenge of establishing a standard format for human-written service descriptions. This approach surpasses our previous work in sentence accuracy and enables the rapid construction of prompts that are more comprehensible than those generated by our prior rule-based design. Furthermore, we have conducted extensive experiments on extracting service demand through LLMs fine-tuning and have developed generalized, effective, and efficient prompts suitable for this process. Our approach outperforms the original LLMs version, achieving superior results.

The rest of the paper is organized as follows: In Section 2, we define the problem addressed in the paper. Section 3 reviews the related work in the literature. Section 4 explains our proposed approach in detail. Section 5 presents our experimental results and includes a discussion of these findings. Finally, we conclude our work in Section 6.

2 Related Work

The primary concern and target of most surveyed ASC studies is to fulfill user requests or service requirements. User requests, expressed in natural language, typically do not conform to a specific format. Therefore, the most critical task is converting these requests into uniform service requirements. A service requirement is composed of two parts: the non-functional requirements and the functional expressions. Y. Fanjiang et al. [3] concluded that most existing ASC approaches and studies assume tuple-based service demands as the working input for subsequent service composition procedures. A generic tuple-based service description model (template) as defined in [3] is as follows:

$$<\mathrm{I, O, P, E, NF, ON}>$$

where I, O, P, E, and NF represent the input, output, precondition, effect, and nonfunctional property sets of a described service, respectively, and ON connects to a knowledge ontology that formally and semantically defines the elements contained in the other tuples [3].

The goal of composing disparate service requirements into a specific tuple-based format introduces several research challenges. First, it necessitates the identification of clear requirement types from a software engineering perspective. Second, these approaches must accurately recognize the textual requirements. Finally, these methods can efficiently extract target components from textual content. This section provides an overview of relevant studies in these research domains.

Rule-based knowledge extraction remains a viable approach due to its reliance on predefined rules that establish relationships between manual documents and tuple-based requirements. In previous work [14], [15], specific rules related to word positioning within requirement descriptions were identified through detailed analysis. Additionally, the NLP tool Stanford CoreNLP [8] was employed to parse and tag a dataset composed of sentences from the LeetCode website. This process involved the development of a part-of-speech (POS) tagger, which assigns parts of speech-such as nouns, verbs, and adjectives-to each word in the text. The grammatical structure revealed by these tags facilitated the creation of rules for more complex cases, particularly for sentences that did not belong to critical sets. Consequently, these structured rules enabled the extraction of target words across different classifications.

Machine learning-based knowledge extraction is favored for its potential to achieve higher performance than traditional methods. Miwa et al. [9] proposed using LSTM-RNNs to enable the simultaneous extraction of entities and relations. Zhang et al. designed a holon ontology structure and selected RoBERTa-base-SQuAD2[3] [18], a pre-trained model utilizing the Robustly Optimized BERT Approach (RoBERTa) [7]. Using this model, they converted raw data into a holon description in JSON format, which was then transformed into a holon class. This process resulted in unified format information that could be easily recognized by their IoT devices. Recently, LLMs, such as BERT [2], BART [5], T5 [13], Llama 2 [16], and GPT [1,11,12], have come to dominate the field of question answering due to their ability to generate effective responses. Consequently, we aim to leverage the capabilities of these LLMs to build an automated workflow for service demand extraction.

3 Problem

This section defines the investigated service composition problem and its motivation. ASC research necessitates significant resources for formalizing requirement texts, mainly since software engineering professionals are tasked with analyzing human-expressed content and transforming it into high-quality system design specifications. In this study, we utilize LeetCode [4], which offers numerous functional descriptions. Each description suggests the *Input* and *Output* of a desired software component, closely mirroring service requirements and serving as our primary source for natural language-based service demands. We provide one clear illustration of this with the following textual description example, collected in our new dataset (discussed in Subsect. 4.1):

> *A problem from LeetCode is presented as follows:*
> *"You are given a string s and an integer k. You can choose any character of the string and change it to any other uppercase English character. You can perform this operation at most k times. Return the length of the longest substring containing the same letter you can get after performing the above operations."*

Expanding on service requirements, we convert the above textual description into a tuple-based format for ASC-compliant formalization. As in our previous work [14], to facilitate performance comparison with standards, the remainder of this paper will focus on and report the handling of *Input* and *Output* tuples. The following example illustrates this process:

> *The nonfunctional requirement with ASC-compliant formalization:*
> $< I = (astrings; anintegerk,$
> $O = (thelengthofthelongestsubstring) >$

Based on the above discussion, a crucial step towards achieving ASC is the transformation of textual expressions by humans into a specific, uniform format. Approaches that enable precise extraction can effectively address this challenge. Thus, we can define and formally formulate the problem as follows:

$$LLM(\bar{X} \rightarrow \bar{Y}) \rightarrow F, and \quad then \quad F : X \rightarrow Y \tag{1}$$

where LLM denotes an LLM used in this study to train and obtain an extraction model F for ASC; X and Y represent a set of human-expressed service demands and a set of corresponding tuple-based demands for X, respectively; $\bar{X}$ and $\bar{Y}$ denote sets of training cases that simulate text for service demands for LLM's fine-tuning and their corresponding tuple-based elements, respectively, where $\bar{X} \subseteq X$ and $\bar{Y} \subseteq Y$. In essence, our goal is to find a valid function F using $LLM()$ to map $\bar{X}$ to $\bar{Y}$, aiming for high-precision extraction. This study focuses on the $LLM()$ design, selecting and comparing mainstream LLM for precise extraction.

4 Approach

In this study, we face several challenges, including the scarcity of service demand data sources and the accuracy of extracting tuple-based service demand information. To address these issues, we will first focus on collecting suitable data.

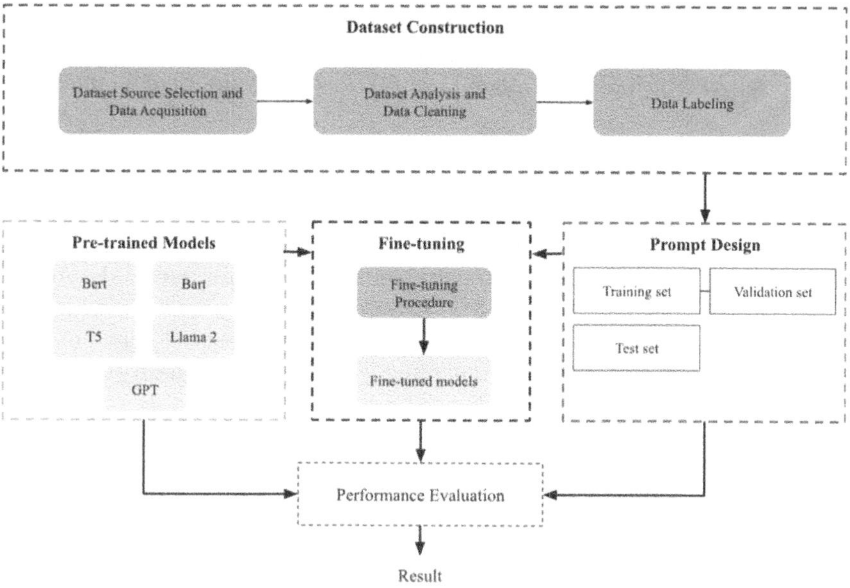

Fig. 1. Workflow of our approach

Subsequently, we will analyze various LLMs to select the most appropriate model and design for our objectives. The overall workflow is depicted in Fig. 1.

4.1 Dataset Construction

Dataset Source Selection and Data Acquisition. In our initial research phase, we sought human-written ASC requests from the existing literature. However, we found only a limited number of sentences that require more diversity and volume for our study. The challenge consists of many datasets containing undefined inputs and outputs, complex formatting symbols, and elements not aligning with our research requirements.

To address these challenges, selecting LeetCode as our dataset source is a reasonable choice [14]. LeetCode provides a wealth of functional descriptions, each detailing the input and output requirements of software components. These descriptions closely resemble service requirements, offering a rich corpus of natural language-based data for our analysis. In contrast to a previous dataset we analyzed, which contained only 170 entries and lacked comprehensiveness, we expanded our data collection by gathering a new, more extensive dataset of functional descriptions from LeetCode.

Dataset Analysis and Data Cleaning. This methodology ensures we have a comprehensive, detailed dataset for analyzing and extracting tuple-based service demands from natural language descriptions. It also sets a robust foundation for further analysis and model development.

Our dataset, derived from LeetCode's extensive collection of 3,017 programming challenges, consists of a selected subset of 500 problems. This sample was randomly selected to balance manual annotation and analytical representativeness.

After a thorough examination, we found specific categories that did not align with our research objectives. Specifically, we excluded problems labeled as 'Database' due to their unique format, which frequently incorporates nonstandard descriptions and SQL table schemas, elements that cannot be directly translated into the general service requirements essential for our study. Additionally, we removed entries featuring inconsistent HTML structures, which posed challenges for accurate parsing. This selection process ensured that our dataset remained focused and relevant to our aims, enhancing the quality and applicability of our research.

The initial dataset encompassed 88.56% of LeetCode's problem diversity. After excluding problems labeled as 'Database', which accounted for 8.19% of LeetCode's problem diversity due to their unique formats, the focus was narrowed to 57 categories. This adjustment resulted in covering 96.46% of the remaining diversity of LeetCode's problems.

This adjustment ensured the integrity and consistency of our dataset, preserving a broad spectrum of programming and algorithmic challenges while aligning more closely with our study's focus on accurate service demand information.

Data Labeling. A pivotal step in refining our dataset for analysis involved manually annotating the I and O tuples, representing *Input* and *Output*, for each problem description. This meticulous process was essential in transforming raw problem descriptions into structured data, facilitating the training and evaluation of our models.

We ensured high accuracy and consistency in our dataset by assigning three annotators to independently label all 500 entries with *Input* and *Output* tuples. This comprehensive approach allowed for the examination of each data point from multiple perspectives. Following the initial annotation, an expert in software engineering reviewed the labels to identify and resolve discrepancies among the annotators, thereby achieving consensus on the most accurate labels for each entry.

This rigorous and collaborative annotation process ensured high reliability in our dataset, which is crucial for the effectiveness of our study. The meticulous attention to detail during the data labeling stage provided a robust foundation for our research, facilitating the development and assessment of our models. This dataset collection process is a cornerstone of our study, enabling the creation and evaluation of models designed to extract service demands. The following entries are formatted according to the processes described above:

- **ID:** A unique identifier for each problem allows us to easily reference and organize the dataset.
- **URL:** The direct link to the problem on LeetCode provides a pathway to view the original problem context and details.

- **Sentence (Original):** The problem description as it appears on LeetCode, including HTML tags. This version preserves the original formatting and structure, which is essential for understanding the context and specifics of each problem.
- **Sentence (Processed):** The problem description, after removing extraneous information such as HTML tags, focuses solely on the textual content. This cleaned version enhances accessibility for analysis and processing.
- **Label (Main):** The service demand pertains to the *Input* or *Output* in the processed content. It is important to note that there can be multiple instances of service demand information.

4.2 Pre-trained Models Vs. Fine-Tuning

In recent years, various LLMs have achieved high performance in natural language processing fields. To popularize our approach, we aim to select LLMs that can work effectively and efficiently with limited computational resources and data. Consequently, we chose indicative LLMs such as BERT, BART, T5, Llama 2, and GPT due to their outstanding pre-trained model performance.

Given the substantial resources required to retrain a new LLM, two mainstream approaches have been developed to achieve task-specific goals in natural language processing [6].

The first approach involves leveraging pre-trained models without additional training or fine-tuning on a specific dataset. This method is prevalent in LLMs, where the model is applied to a task without prior exposure to task-specific data, relying solely on its pre-existing knowledge-examples include zero-shot learning. Alternatively, the model can provide one or more examples of task-specific data to improve performance, as demonstrated in one-shot and few-shot learning. These approaches enable LLMs to generate accurate responses while conserving computational resources and minimizing the time required for fine-tuning. Additionally, they reduce the need for large amounts of labeled data.

The second approach entails fine-tuning pre-trained models on a specific dataset tailored to the task at hand. In this approach, the model undergoes additional training with a substantial amount of task-specific data, allowing its parameters to be refined and optimized for the target task. This method enables LLMs to achieve high accuracy in task-specific applications while also reducing the substantial resource requirements associated with training a new LLM from scratch.

Due to computational cost considerations, we initially employed zero-shot, one-shot, and few-shot learning methods, as these approaches can significantly reduce the time required for model tuning. However, our experiments revealed that existing LLMs exhibited limited performance on the specific service demand extraction task when relying solely on pre-trained models without fine-tuning. Consequently, we proceeded to fine-tune the pre-trained model using our training dataset. During the fine-tuning process, we aimed to minimize the discrepancy between the instance's label and the LLM's extracted output. In the testing phase, we concatenated the instruction designed for the service demand task with

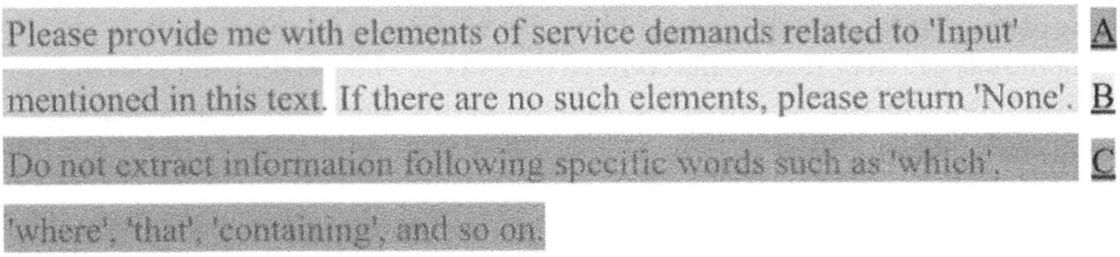

Fig. 2. Prompt Design

the relevant information and the human-expressed textual data. This integrated input is then fed into the LLMs to extract the service demand. Further details on this procedure will be discussed in the following section.

4.3 Prompt Design

Creating an appropriate prompt is one of the most critical tasks in leveraging LLMs. Mainstream LLMs are typically applied to general question-and-answer tasks rather than specific tasks such as service demand analysis. Therefore, the quality of this study heavily depends on the amount of information provided and the precision of the prompt design.

In our observation, we encountered three main issues affecting the accuracy of extracting service demand through GPT. First, the common keyword extraction tasks following the prompt principles outlined in [10] are not appropriate for specific tasks. Standard prompts for keyword extraction often fail to precisely capture service demand information, instead retrieving extraneous details. Second, people's descriptions of their needs do not always contain explicit service demand information regarding *Input* or *Output*. Therefore, it is a challenge to ensure the model returns correct information when no explicit service demand is present. Finally, individuals often include extraneous expressions surrounding the service demand information, which are not the target of our extraction process. Thus, it is crucial to develop prompts that accurately extract only the key information.

To address the aforementioned challenges, we have structured our prompt into three distinct parts to enhance the accuracy of extracting service demands. A prompt can include instructions or questions directed to the model, along with additional elements such as context, inputs, or instances. By incorporating these components, we can more effectively guide the model, thereby improving the quality of the results. Following this principle, the prompt design is divided into three components: Part A provides clear instructions for the service demand extraction task, Part B specifies the response format when the context does not contain any service demand, and Part C focuses the response on extracting specific segments of the text (see Fig. 2).

In part A, we replace the standard prompt example [10], which typically extracts keywords from a block of text, with more precise instructions. Using the term *Extract* in the prompt could lead the LLM to extract general keywords rather than specific service demands. To mitigate this issue, we use alternative verbs such as "provide" and "show," and include a tip indicating that the task involves identifying a specific type of service demand.

In part B, we consider how the LLM should respond when no service demand is present in the textual requirements. Therefore, we design the prompt to account for these scenarios by specifying the output "None" when the text does not contain any service demand. This fixed-format simplifies subsequent data processing.

In part C, the presence of inessential information surrounding the correct service demand can complicate downstream data processing. We observed that such extraneous information often appears near specific words. To address this, we include related words in our prompt to ensure that only the necessary service demand information is extracted. Our experiments demonstrate that replacing the verb "extract" with other related words in this third part does not negatively impact performance.

5 Performance Evaluation

In this section, we first describe our experimental setup, including detailed descriptions of our dataset, hardware, and software configurations. Our goal is to ensure that the experiments conducted can be easily replicated by other researchers. Secondly, we illustrate the evaluation metrics used for evaluating each model.

5.1 Experimental Setup

This subsection introduces our dataset preparation, environment setup, and the procedure for LLMs.

We have systematically prepared our experimental dataset to ensure our model's performance is robust and generalizable. The dataset consists of 500 entries dedicated to exploring the extraction of tuple-based service demands utilizing LLMs. This dataset, primarily sourced from LeetCode, has been enriched with manual annotations of *Input* and *Output* tuples, as discussed in Subsect. 4.1. To eliminate any potential bias introduced by the original order of the data, we shuffled the entries to randomize the order. Subsequently, we divided the dataset into three segments: 64% for the training phase, 16% for the validation phase, and 20% for the testing phase.

Our environment setup is divided into two parts: firstly, we demonstrate that LLMs can operate on a standalone computer, implying that tuple elements can be extracted using minimal resources; secondly, we aim to achieve optimal performance by running the LLMs online. The related setup details are listed below:

- For the standalone computer environment: Operating System: Ubuntu 22.04 LTS; CPU: Intel Core i9-13900K; GPU: NVIDIA GeForce RTX 4090 24GB;

Memory: 64GB DDR5. The models used for fine-tuning include bert-base-uncased, bart-large, t5-large, and Llama-2-7b-chat-hf.
- For the online environment: We utilize the OpenAI fine-tuning API with the model gpt-3.5-turbo-0613 and gpt-4-turbo.

The fine-tuning procedure varied slightly due to each model's distinct capabilities and architectures. Using a classification approach, BERT was fine-tuned for a keyword extraction task within a QA framework. In contrast, BART, T5, and Llama 2 were treated as sequence-to-sequence (seq2seq) tasks, aligning with their capabilities for generating text outputs from input sequences. This differentiation underlines the versatility and adaptability of modern seq2seq models for complex NLP tasks such as keyword extraction from questions.

Utilizing the online OpenAI GPT API for zero-shot, few-shot, and fine-tuning learning necessitates converting our dataset into the chat-completion JSON format with quality prompts, as discussed in Subsect. 4.2. During fine-tuning, we monitor various metrics, including training set loss and training set accuracy, to adjust hyperparameters. In our experiments, we achieved optimal results with $n\_epochs = 3$ to 5.

5.2 Evaluation Metrics

This subsection describes the evaluation metrics used to assess the models' performance. Accurately extracting all correct fragments that correspond to the context is crucial for extracting the target content for a tuple-based request. Therefore, our primary focus is on evaluating the accuracy of the extracted complete content.

In addition to assessing the completeness of the extracted content, we aim to evaluate the models' performance across various scenarios. These scenarios include instances where a context is associated with multiple labels, lacks an existing label, or has a single label that the model accurately predicts. Consequently, we define common scenarios regarding extraction results corresponding to the classification in the confusion matrix as follows:

- True Positive: In this scenario, for a given description or sentence, the tuple elements extracted by the Approach must exactly correspond to the manually annotated tuple elements of the description (i.e., the correct answers). In this study, we classify a result in this category based on whether the extractions made by the Approach closely match the tuple elements we have labeled.
- False Positive: This scenario is also referred to as a Type-1 Error. In such cases, for a given description, the Approach extracts tuple elements that do not appear in the corresponding ground truth annotation, adversely affecting its judgment of correctness. Additionally, this category encompasses situations where the Approach retrieves correct elements along with redundant segments or elements, impairing its judgment's accuracy.
- True Negative: No elements should be extracted from a description in this scenario, and the Approach correctly retrieves nothing.

- False Negative: This scenario is also referred to as a Type-2 Error. It occurs when the Approach fails to extract the intended tuple elements from a description, resulting in classification into this category. Furthermore, this category encompasses situations where the Approach extracts correct elements with insufficient details, rendering the retrieved tuple elements ambiguous or unclear.

We evaluate each tuple element we have labeled when assessing the set of elements predicted by the Approach. A service description set may be classified into different error types if extractions are incorrect (e.g., a service description with two labels: one label, which the Approach predicts correctly, is classified as True Positive; the other, which the Approach fails to predict, is classified as False Negative). This evaluation metric offers two advantages: first, it allows us to assess the accuracy of every label; second, it enables us to identify significant partitions from which we aim to extract tuple elements.

5.3 Result and Discussion

Table 1. The performance of zero-shot, one-shot, and few-shot (10 cases) learning is evaluated based on the accuracy of sentence extraction for the *Input* and *Output* tuple types. These evaluations is conducted using the GPT-4 model.

Method	Accuracy Input	Accuracy Output
Zero-shot learning	0.00	0.11
One-shot learning	0.01	0.34
Few-shot learning	0.66	0.60

Table 2. The performance of few-shot learning (10 cases) and fine-tuning is evaluated based on the time required to extract both the *Input* and *Output* tuple types from the test cases. For these evaluations, we employed a few-shot learning approach using the GPT-4 model and a fine-tuned approach using the GPT-3.5 model.

Method	Time(s) Input	Time(s) Output
Zero-shot learning	153	172
One-shot learning	154	192
Few-shot learning	185	231
Fine-tuning	92	85

Performance of the Pre-trained Model. In recent years, LLMs have begun to dominate many natural language processing tasks. It is widely recognized that a single pre-trained LLM can be applied to various natural language tasks without fine-tuning. Initially, we present the results of utilizing a pre-trained model without fine-tuning to achieve our goals (see Fig. 2).

We observed poor performance when directly extracting service demand through the pre-trained GPT-4 without any training set information (i.e., zero-shot learning) (see Table 1). Upon examining the extracted segments, we found that the original model did not adequately identify what constituted service demand information. Instead, it tended to display its inference procedure and the answer. Since the model lacked knowledge about service demand, it frequently inferred the answer as "None," as shown below:

> The text does not explicitly mention any elements related to 'Input' in terms of service demands. It only describes a problem scenario involving an array of strings and the process of deleting characters from specific indices to achieve a desired order. Therefore, the answer is 'None'.

However, for the purpose of ASC, we need to obtain clearer service demand segments to efficiently produce the subsequent service composition. A series of intermediate reasoning steps significantly improves the ability of large language models to perform complex reasoning [17]. We designed the reasoning instructions using our training set information to help the LLM understand which parts we want to extract as service demands (i.e., one-shot learning or few-shot learning). We observed improved performance compared to zero-shot learning (see Table 1).

In our observations, performance improves significantly when the training set increases to 10 cases. The segments extracted by the LLM become clearer and more accurate for the service demand information we need. The redundant step-by-step inferences gradually disappear, resulting in impressive performance without fine-tuning the pre-trained GPT-4. However, increasing the amount of training data in the instructions is not an ideal approach, as it requires the model to scan more phases before answering each testing question, thereby wasting computational resources and increasing response time (see Table 2). Therefore, we employed the fine-tuning method in the subsequent phase.

Table 3. The performance of our designed prompt is compared to that of a standard extraction task prompt [10], with evaluations based on the accuracy of sentence extraction for both the *Input* and *Output* tuple types.

Model	Prompt	Accuracy Input	Accuracy Output
Few-shot learning	Standard	0.20	0.21
	Designed	0.66	0.60
Fine-tuning	Standard	0.94	0.96
	Designed	0.97	0.98

Comparison of Designed Prompt and Standard Prompt. Our experiments revealed that prompt design plays a critical role in the performance of LLMs. In Sect. 4.3, we detail our approach to creating an effective prompt, developed through iterative testing with various placeholders and official prompts. We observed that a standard prompt typically used for extraction tasks is insufficient for specific tasks such as our service demand research, particularly when the pre-trained model has not been fine-tuned for this specific task. However, by employing a designed prompt, we achieved an accuracy improvement of over 40% in few-shot learning using the pre-trained model (see Table 3).

Even after fine-tuning the pre-trained model to incorporate knowledge specific to the service demand task, we observed further performance improvements when utilizing our designed prompt. Specifically, there was a notable increase in accuracy when avoiding generic keywords such as "Extract," which are typically employed in standard extraction tasks. Remarkably, we achieved 100% accuracy in cases where no service demand was present, and the extracted service information consistently excluded any redundant segments following the words specified in the prompt. These findings highlight the critical importance of excluding generic terms and incorporating task-specific information into the prompt design.

Table 4. The performance of all models was evaluated based on the accuracy of sentence extraction related to both the *Input* and *Output* tuple types.

Model (Parameter size)	Accuracy Input	Accuracy Output
Rule-based [14]	0.56	0.48
BERT (336M)	0.63	0.67
BART (406M)	0.80	0.61
T5 (770M)	0.89	0.89
Llama 2 (7B)	0.91	0.93
GPT-3.5 (175B)	0.97	0.98

Table 5. The performance of all models is evaluated based on the accuracy of label extraction concerning the *Input* tuple type.

Model	Accuracy	Precision	Recall	F1-score
Rule-based [14]	0.418	0.528	0.667	0.589
BERT	0.529	0.74	0.649	0.692
BART	0.702	0.844	0.807	0.825
T5	0.823	0.911	0.895	0.903
Llama 2	0.861	0.929	0.921	0.925
GPT-3.5	0.957	0.982	0.974	0.978

Table 6. The performance of all models is evaluated based on the accuracy of label extraction concerning the *Output* tuple type.

Model	Accuracy	Precision	Recall	F1-score
Rule-based [14]	0.379	0.500	0.500	0.500
BERT	0.591	0.788	0.703	0.743
BART	0.522	0.691	0.631	0.66
T5	0.84	0.918	0.891	0.904
Llama 2	0.912	0.969	0.93	0.949
GPT-3.5	0.982	1.00	0.980	0.990

Performance of Fine-Tuning. Using evaluation metrics based on a set of descriptions or tuples, we employed the related work [14], which utilizes a rule-based approach, as the baseline model for comparison. We then assessed the performance of various fine-tuned LLMs, including BERT, BART, T5, Llama 2, and GPT-3.5, against this baseline.

In the analysis of accuracy for each service demand candidate (see Table 4), a score is assigned only when the fine-tuned model correctly predicts all elements of the service demand for each description. This stringent criterion ensures that the reported accuracy reflects the model's ability to fully capture the necessary details of the service demand in each case. We observed that the rule-based approach, when applied with initial rules, is less effective on larger-scale datasets compared to its performance on the original dataset. Specifically, the rule-based method requires additional rule-setting to achieve higher performance on larger datasets. This task of identifying suitable rules demands substantial human effort from ASC experts.

Furthermore, in our analysis of the accuracy for each service demand candidate, a score is given when the fine-tuned model correctly predicts every element of the service demand for each description (see Tables 5 and 6. We observed that fine-tuned LLMs achieve high precision, enabling the extraction of correct elements while rarely producing non-existent ones. This precision is crucial in preventing the generation of misleading elements that could be difficult for humans to distinguish.

In contrast, the other LLM approaches consistently outperformed the rule-based methods. Our experiments demonstrate that the model's parameter size significantly impacts performance across different models (see Table 4). A similar trend was observed in the evaluation of each service demand candidate (see Tables 5 and 6.

Our GPT-3.5 fine-tuning model, augmented with prompt design (see Subsect. 4.2), demonstrates outstanding performance regardless of whether the evaluation metric is based on a set of descriptions or a tuple from a set, and irrespective of whether the tuple elements are *Input* or *Output*; it nearly achieved all correct answers. This demonstrates that GPT-3.5, when fine-tuned with effectively designed prompts leveraging knowledge from our dataset, represents a highly flexible approach to addressing the problem defined in Sect. 3. Moreover, it is more efficient compared to GPT-4 with few-shot learning during the extraction of service demands from the testing set, saving half the cost and about 2 times faster while achieving greater accuracy (see Table 2). An additional advantage of GPT-3.5 became evident during fine-tuning and the extraction of tuple elements: it can automatically correct mistakes, such as grammatical errors, that were inadvertently introduced in our labels. This capability is not present in rule-based approaches. With this advantage, we can more accurately extract tuple-based service demands for ASC.

6 Conclusion

ASC approaches typically require inputs in a specifically designated tuple-based format, presenting several challenges. Our study introduces a representative dataset we collected, along with reasoning designs and strategies for LLMs, such as appropriate prompt design, and a detailed few-shot learning and fine-tuning process. Compared to our previous rule-based approach, the LLM strategies accommodate greater complexity and scale more effectively to new datasets. We demonstrate that our approach can efficiently and effectively extract accurate tuple-based service demands for ASC.

In addition to the *Input* and *Output* tuple types, there are other functional and nonfunctional property sets of a described service. In the future, we plan to enhance our approach by including various tuple types such as precondition and postcondition. By achieving complete extraction with tuple-based approaches, a higher level of automation can be attained, reducing human intervention and improving the productivity of ASC.

Acknowledgments. This work was partially supported by the National Science and Technology Council, Taiwan, under Grant No. NSTC112-2221-E-001-008. We thank Ming-To Chuang, an intern research assistant at the National Taiwan University, Department of Electrical Engineering, for his valuable assistance with our dataset construction.

References

1. Brown, T., et al.: Language models are few-shot learners. In: Larochelle, H., Ranzato, M., Hadsell, R., Balcan, M., Lin, H. (eds.) Advances in Neural Information Processing Systems, vol. 33, pp. 1877–1901. Curran Associates, Inc. (2020)
2. Devlin, J., Chang, M.W., Lee, K., Toutanova, K.: BERT: pre-training of deep bidirectional transformers for language understanding. arXiv preprint arXiv:1810.04805 (2018). https://arxiv.org/abs/1810.04805
3. Fanjiang, Y., Syu, Y., Ma, S., Kuo, J.: An overview and classification of service description approaches in automated service composition research. IEEE Trans. Serv. Comput. **10**(02), 176–189 (2017). https://doi.org/10.1109/TSC.2015.2461538
4. https://leetcode.com/problemset/, online

5. Lewis, M., et al.: BART: denoising sequence-to-sequence pre-training for natural language generation, translation, and comprehension. arXiv arXiv preprint arXiv:1910.13461 (2019). https://arxiv.org/abs/1910.13461
6. Liu, H., et al.: Few-shot parameter-efficient fine-tuning is better and cheaper than in-context learning. In: Koyejo, S., Mohamed, S., Agarwal, A., Belgrave, D., Cho, K., Oh, A. (eds.) Advances in Neural Information Processing Systems, vol. 35, pp. 1950–1965. Curran Associates, Inc. (2022). https://proceedings.neurips.cc/paper_files/paper/2022/file/0cde695b83bd186c1fd456302888454c-Paper-Conference.pdf
7. Liu, Y., et al.: RoBERTa: a robustly optimized BERT pretraining approach (2019)
8. Manning, C.D., Surdeanu, M., Bauer, J., Finkel, J., Bethard, S.J., McClosky, D.: The Stanford CoreNLP natural language processing toolkit. In: Association for Computational Linguistics (ACL) System Demonstrations, pp. 55–60 (2014). http://www.aclweb.org/anthology/P/P14/P14-5010
9. Miwa, M., Bansal, M.: End-to-end relation extraction using LSTMs on sequences and tree structures. In: Erk, K., Smith, N.A. (eds.) Proceedings of the 54th Annual Meeting of the Association for Computational Linguistics (Volume 1: Long Papers). pp. 1105–1116. Association for Computational Linguistics, Berlin, Germany (2016). https://doi.org/10.18653/v1/P16-1105, https://aclanthology.org/P16-1105
10. https://platform.openai.com/docs/guides/, online
11. Radford, A., Narasimhan, K., Salimans, T., Sutskever, I., et al.: Improving language understanding by generative pre-training (2018). work in progress
12. Radford, A., Wu, J., Child, R., Luan, D., Amodei, D., Sutskever, I., et al.: Language models are unsupervised multitask learners. OpenAI blog **1**(8), 9 (2019)
13. Raffel, C., et al.: Exploring the limits of transfer learning with a unified text-to-text transformer. In: arXiv preprint arXiv:1910.10683. arXiv, arXiv (Oct 2019), https://arxiv.org/abs/1910.10683
14. Syu, Y., Tsao, Y.J., Wang, C.M.: Rule-based extraction of tuple-based service demand from natural language-based software requirement for automated service composition. In: Katangur, A., Zhang, L.J. (eds.) Services Computing - SCC 2021, pp. 1–17. Springer International Publishing, Cham (2022). https://doi.org/10.1007/978-3-030-96566-2_1
15. Syu, Y., Wang, C.M.: A gap between automated service composition research and software engineering development practice: Service descriptions. In: Zhang, Y., Zhang, L.J. (eds.) Web Services - ICWS 2023, pp. 18–31. Springer Nature Switzerland, Cham (2023). https://doi.org/10.1007/978-3-031-44836-2_2
16. Touvron, H., Martin, L., Stone, K., et al.: Llama 2: open foundation and fine-tuned chat models. arXiv arXiv:2307.09288 (2023). https://arxiv.org/abs/2307.09288
17. Wei, J., et al.: Chain-of-thought prompting elicits reasoning in large language models. In: Proceedings of the 36th International Conference on Neural Information Processing Systems, NIPS 2022, Curran Associates Inc., Red Hook, NY, USA (2024)
18. Zhang, Z., Elkhatib, Y., Elhabbash, A.: NLP-based generation of ontological system descriptions for composition of smart home devices. In: 2023 IEEE International Conference on Web Services (ICWS), pp. 360–370 (2023). https://doi.org/10.1109/ICWS60048.2023.00055

Revolutionizing Pharmaceutical Integrity: Using Smart Contracts and NFT Encryption to Safeguard Against Counterfeit Drugs

Khanh H. V.[1], Triet M. N.[1(✉)], Hung N. N.[1], Bang N. H.[1], Trinh P. D.[1], Khoa T. D.[1], Ngan K. T. N.[2], and Anh N. T[1]

[1] FPT University, Can Tho, Vietnam
{khanhvh,trietnm3}@fe.edu.vn
[2] FPT Polytecnic, Can Tho, Vietnam

Abstract. The pharmaceutical industry is challenged by issues of transparency, traceability, and integrity within its global supply chain. Traditional methods have often been inadequate in addressing these concerns, which are crucial for maintaining ethical standards and ensuring consumer trust. This paper proposes a novel system utilizing blockchain technology, smart contracts, encrypted Non-Fungible Tokens (NFTs), and the InterPlanetary File System (IPFS) to enhance the management of pharmaceutical supply chains. By incorporating these technologies, our framework seeks to improve transparency and data integrity from the source to the consumer. We also evaluate the application of six encryption algorithms—RSA, RC4, DES, ChaCha20, Blowfish, and AES-to determine the best balance between security and efficiency. This system has been tested on four EVM-compatible platforms: Binance Smart Chain, Polygon, Fantom, and Celo, assessing its adaptability and operational efficiency. The results indicate that our approach not only meets the stringent requirements of the pharmaceutical sector but also establishes a reliable, transparent, and equitable supply chain system.

Keywords: Pharmaceuticals Supply Chain · Supply Chain Transparency · Fair Trade · Blockchain Technology · Smart Contracts · NFTs · IPFS · Distributed Ledger · Ethical Sourcing

1 Introduction

The pharmaceutical industry faces ongoing challenges in maintaining transparency, ethical sourcing, and integrity within its global supply chain. Traditional methods often fall short in achieving the required levels of traceability and transparency, which are essential for upholding ethical standards and securing consumer trust. Each phase of the conventional supply chain [6], from production to distribution, is susceptible to issues that can compromise both integrity

S. He and L.-J. Zhang (Eds.): SCF/SCC 2024, LNCS 15430, pp. 17–32, 2025.
https://doi.org/10.1007/978-3-031-77000-5_2

and transparency [9]. The application of blockchain technology, along with smart contracts, encrypted Non-Fungible Tokens (NFTs), and the InterPlanetary File System (IPFS), provides a viable method to overcome these challenges. By integrating these technologies, we propose a tailored supply chain management system [8] for the pharmaceutical industry, designed to improve transparency and ensure data integrity from the source to the consumer [14,15].

Recent research has focused on enhancing the integrity of pharmaceutical supply chains through the adoption of blockchain technology. Various blockchain-based frameworks have been developed to address the critical problem of counterfeit drugs, ensuring both traceability and security of pharmaceutical transactions [22,27]. Noteworthy initiatives include the blockchain-enabled Medledger system, aimed at securing drug supply chain transactions, and solutions that utilize the Ethereum blockchain to monitor counterfeit drugs while incorporating IPFS for better data storage [27]. Additionally, there has been significant analysis of blockchain and IoT-based systems for supply chain management, with a focus on enhancing transparency, traceability, and security [18,23]. These efforts underline a growing consensus on the capacity of blockchain and associated technologies to substantially improve pharmaceutical supply chain management, aiming to establish a system characterized by enhanced transparency, efficiency, and stakeholder trust.

Our strategy enhances the pharmaceutical supply chain management by implementing smart contracts, encrypted NFTs, IPFS, and distributed ledgers to establish a robust system that guarantees data integrity and transparency from the point of origin to the consumer. To achieve this, we have tested six different encryption algorithms-RSA, RC4, DES, ChaCha20, Blowfish, and AES-to identify the optimal balance between security and operational efficiency. This method not only securely tracks the journey of pharmaceutical products but also addresses the specific challenges of traceability and ethical sourcing crucial in this sector. Our approach, informed by the scalability and data integrity needs identified by Pawar et al. and the trust and authenticity concerns noted by Hawashin et al. [11,20], ensures the selection of the most suitable encryption algorithm through rigorous evaluation. By doing so, our blockchain-based framework provides a dependable record of all transactions, allowing all participants in the supply chain access to consistent, real-time, and accurate information, thus fostering a transparent, adaptable, and equitable pharmaceutical supply chain system.

The performance and adaptability of our proposed system were tested on four EVM-compatible platforms: Binance Smart Chain, Polygon, Fantom, and Celo. This evaluation demonstrated the system's flexibility and its ability to utilize the unique features of each platform to enhance supply chain management. Essential operations such as data logging, NFT generation, and NFT transferability were tested, providing insights into the system's capabilities concerning speed, efficiency, and reliability. Moreover, an economic evaluation, comparing transaction fees across these platforms, supported our system's potential for cost savings and improved operational efficiency.

In conclusion, our research delivers a comprehensive and structured model that employs blockchain technology, smart contracts, encrypted NFTs, and IPFS to transform supply chain management practices within the pharmaceutical sector. This model addresses critical issues such as transparency, efficiency, and ethical sourcing, thereby setting a new benchmark for supply chain operations. Through meticulous implementation, thorough evaluation, and a focus on economic viability, our findings underscore the significant role these technologies could play in fostering a supply chain environment characterized by fairness, transparency, and trust.

2 Related Work

2.1 Sustainable Supply Chain and Transparency

Recent developments in the pharmaceutical supply chain have seen the introduction of blockchain-based solutions aimed at reducing the incidence of counterfeit drugs and improving the traceability and security of drug transactions. Uddin (2021) developed the Medledger system, which utilizes Hyperledger Fabric to facilitate secure transactions in drug supply chains [27]. Rai, Srivastava, and Arora (2023) examined the use of smart contracts on the Ethereum blockchain, coupled with IPFS for data storage, to monitor counterfeit drugs [21]. Similarly, Lingayat et al. (2021) reviewed various blockchain and IoT systems for managing pharmaceutical supply chains, noting the advantages and limitations of these technologies [16]. Amarasinghe et al. (2022) introduced SUPPLYDECK, a blockchain-based solution designed to improve transparency, traceability, and security within drug supply chains [2]. In addition, Musamih et al. (2023) discussed an Ethereum-based system for tracking healthcare supply chain products, which integrates smart contracts and decentralized storage [17]. Furthermore, Gebreab et al. (2022) proposed a system that uses NFTs to manage the traceability and ownership of medical devices in healthcare supply chains [7]. These contributions highlight blockchain's role in enhancing drug authenticity, improving traceability, and securing transactions within the pharmaceutical industry.

2.2 Enhancing Pharmaceutical Supply Chain Integrity Through Blockchain Technology

Recent research highlights the role of blockchain technology in enhancing the pharmaceutical supply chain, particularly in improving drug traceability, security, and combating counterfeit medicines. Haq & Muselemu (2018) discuss the potential of blockchain to monitor pharmaceuticals from production to distribution, aiming to increase transparency [10]. Kumar & Tripathi (2019) explore the use of blockchain combined with encrypted QR codes to improve medication traceability and safety [12]. Bali et al. (2022) investigate how blockchain can help reduce drug counterfeiting by enabling traceable ownership transfers [3]. Kumar et al. (2023) assess various blockchain-based systems for their effectiveness in enhancing pharmaceutical safety and optimizing supply chain processes [13]. Rai, Srivastava, & Arora (2023) detail a decentralized tracking system using smart contracts on the Ethereum blockchain aimed at cost efficiency [22]. Lingayat et al. (2021) compare blockchain and IoT-based systems to enhance safety in pharmaceutical products [16]. Dave et al. (2022) propose a permissioned blockchain network to foster collaboration and trust among supply chain participants [5]. Saindane et al. (2020) use blockchain to increase transparency and reduce counterfeit risks in the drug supply chain [25], while Pathak et al. (2022) and Ali et al. (2022) advocate for blockchain systems that ensure traceable and secure pharmaceutical supply chains [1,19]. These studies collectively emphasize blockchain's utility in ensuring security, authenticity, and traceability in the pharmaceutical supply chain.

2.3 Advancements in Pharmaceutical Supply Chain Security: The Role of IoT and Blockchain

Recent advancements have highlighted the integration of the Internet of Things (IoT) and blockchain technology as a method to improve the security and traceability of the pharmaceutical supply chain. Rayan and Zubair (2021) discuss an IoT-integrated blockchain framework that addresses pharmaceutical counterfeiting and aims to enhance drug supply chain management [23]. Singh, Dwivedi, and Srivastava (2020) focus on an IoT sensor-based blockchain framework designed for monitoring temperature and preventing counterfeit drugs, which is critical for maintaining drug integrity throughout the supply chain [26]. Nawale and Konapure (2021) consider the use of IoT and blockchain for better drug traceability, targeting effective and safe healthcare delivery [18]. Botcha, Chakravarthy, and Anurag (2019) explore ways to improve traceability and efficiency in the pharmaceutical supply chain through the use of IoT devices coupled with blockchain technology, also aiming at enhancing consumer protection [4]. Additionally, S et al. (2023) focus on utilizing blockchain to ensure the quality of medicines, secure transactions, and protect data in the pharmaceutical sector, which contributes to system reliability and mitigates the risks of counterfeit medications [24]. Collectively, these studies point to the potential benefits of merging IoT and blockchain technologies to tackle existing challenges in the pharmaceutical supply chain, emphasizing improved security, traceability, and consumer safety.

3 Approach

3.1 The Classical Architecture of Transparency and Ethical Sourcing in Pharmaceutical Supply Chain Management

The traditional pharmaceutical supply chain is a sequence of essential steps that guide the journey of pharmaceutical products from the collection of raw materials to their final delivery to patients. The process begins with raw material suppliers who provide the necessary components for drug manufacturing, including active pharmaceutical ingredients (APIs) and excipients. These ingredients are fundamental to the creation of any medication. Pharmaceutical companies then take

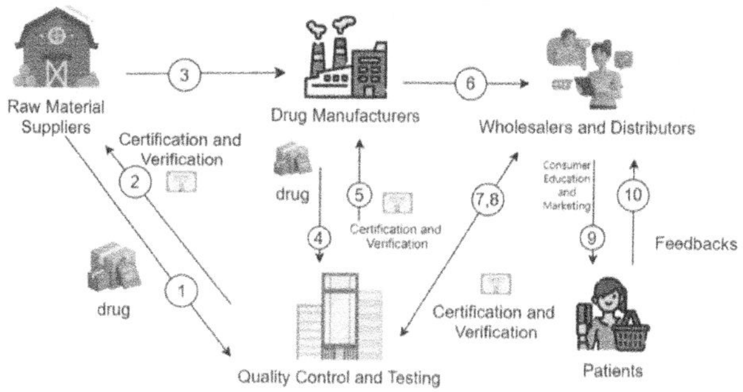

Fig. 1. A Flowchart Depicting the Traditional Management of Pharmaceuticals Supply Chain: From Raw Material Sourcing to Patient Delivery

these materials and proceed with the formulation, production, and packaging of the final drug products, a phase crucial for establishing the overall quality and effectiveness of the medications.

During the manufacturing and distribution stages, a comprehensive system of quality control and testing is implemented. This involves continuous assessments aimed at confirming the safety and effectiveness of the pharmaceutical products. After manufacturing, each batch of drugs undergoes thorough testing to adhere to rigorous safety standards. Subsequent certification and verification processes are carried out to ensure the integrity of these products before they are distributed.

Wholesalers and distributors play a critical role as they acquire medications in large volumes and handle the logistics of delivering them to various healthcare providers, including hospitals and pharmacies. This distribution network is vital for maintaining the integrity of the supply chain, ensuring that medications are delivered to their intended destinations efficiently. At the end of the chain are the patients, whose health depends on the reliability of these processes. The supply chain is completed by gathering consumer feedback and data, which are crucial for ongoing monitoring of the product's performance and safety in actual usage scenarios.

In the pharmaceutical industry, the traditional supply chain management model follows a methodical path from the acquisition of raw materials to the final delivery of products to patients. Despite its systematic approach, this model often struggles with maintaining complete transparency and traceability at various points in the process. A consistent challenge within the supply chain is the adherence to ethical standards, including the assurance of fair trade practices among all stakeholders involved. This issue remains a significant concern, as ensuring fairness and accountability is crucial for the integrity of the supply chain (Fig. 2).

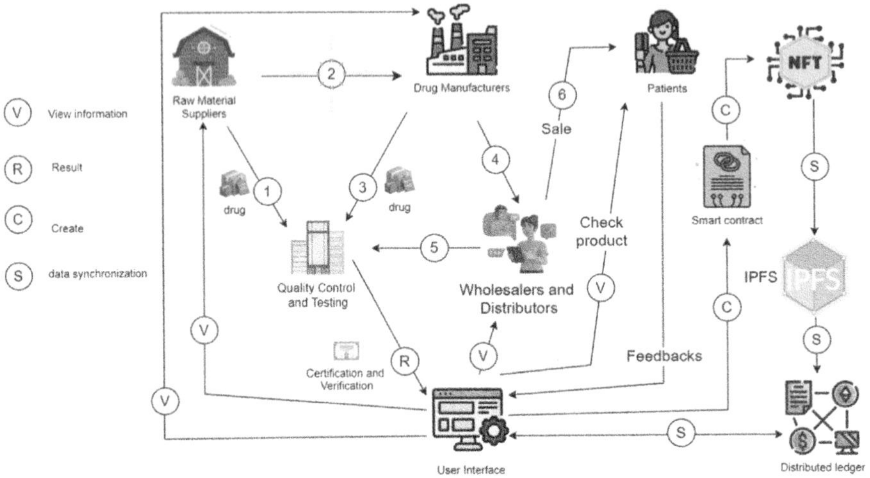

Fig. 2. A Schematic Representation of the Pharmaceuticals Supply Chain Management System Integrating Smart Contracts, NFTs, IPFS, and Distributed Ledgers

3.2 Implementing Blockchain, Smart Contracts, NFTs, and IPFS for Supply Chain Integrity in the Pharmaceutical Sectors

The pharmaceutical supply chain management system outlined in the schematic employs technologies such as Smart Contracts, encrypted NFTs, IPFS, and Distributed Ledgers to ensure the integrity of pharmaceutical products from their origin to the end-user. Initially, raw material suppliers provide the necessary ingredients for drug production, where rigorous quality assurance and authentication of materials are required. As these ingredients are shipped to manufacturers, Smart Contracts facilitate the automation of transactions, confirming that all conditions, including delivery schedules and quality specifications, are adhered to and accurately recorded on a Distributed Ledger.

During the production phase, quality control and testing are critical. They function to confirm the quality of products at several points within the supply chain. The certification and verification processes are securely recorded on the Distributed Ledger, confirming that the drugs meet high health and safety standards. Additionally, each drug package or batch is assigned a unique encrypted NFT, granting it a distinct digital identity that can be traced throughout the supply chain. This feature allows stakeholders, including wholesalers, distributors, and patients, to verify the authenticity of the drug at any point by checking against the immutable records.

Feedback from patients and healthcare providers is collected through interfaces that interact with Distributed Ledgers and IPFS, providing a reliable and transparent record of drug effectiveness and safety after reaching the market. IPFS offers a decentralized storage solution that helps protect critical data throughout the supply chain from tampering and loss. The system ensures synchronicity of data across different platforms, supporting a structured approach to accountability, consistent traceability, and quality assurance. This ensures that patients receive genuine medications, maintaining trust in the pharmaceutical supply chain.

4 Implementation

In the implementation section of our study, we explore the application of various encryption algorithms to secure metadata for Non-Fungible Tokens (NFTs), which are crucial for the blockchain-based pharmaceutical supply chain management system. Our evaluation focuses on the effectiveness of these algorithms in terms of security and time efficiency, essential factors that influence the operational efficiency of the system. Performance metrics, presented in detailed tables, examine how these encryption algorithms perform when securing both image and text data, which are vital for maintaining the transparency of the pharmaceutical supply chain. Within the context of blockchain and smart contract applications, these encryption times provide valuable insights into the feasibility and practical implications of using encrypted NFTs and IPFS data in our system (Table 1).

Table 1. RSA Encryption and Decryption Performance for Image and text Data in Microseconds

RSA	1	2	3	4	5	6	7	8	9	10
Generating key	52175	63937	57903	51487	63256	89990	47233	40353	75905	98625
Encrypting image	10159	11506	7550	6438	9479	1609	6152	6704	10979	10646
Decrypting image	216253	213812	210932	218233	228707	212589	178727	190148	259331	260586
Generating key	47697	42562	62744	78997	59755	74911	80546	92969	46018	82341
Encrypting text	0	0	0	0	0	0	0	0	0	998
Decrypting text	682	0	0	2639	4815	0	0	0	502	0

The table provided details the performance of RSA encryption across a series of operations within a pharmaceutical supply chain integrity system. The data showcases a considerable variance in RSA key generation times, ranging from 40,353 to 98,625 microseconds across different trials, suggesting inconsistent performance. For image data, encryption times were more consistent but varied from as low as 1,609 to as high as 11,506 microseconds, while decryption times were significantly higher, consistently exceeding 178,727 microseconds and reaching up to 260,586 microseconds in some trials. Text data encryption was almost instantaneous in all cases, with negligible times except for one instance of 998 microseconds. Text decryption also showed minimal times, though with occasional spikes, such as 2,639 and 4,815 microseconds. These results, summarized in the table (Fig. 1), highlight RSA's strong security but also reveal its potential limitations in terms of computational efficiency and speed, which could impact its suitability for high-demand environments like pharmaceutical supply chains where rapid data processing is critical.

Table 2. RC4 Encryption and Decryption Performance for Image and text Data in Microseconds

RC4 (image)	1	2	3	4	5	6	7	8	9	10
Encrypting image	0	0	0	0	0	0	0	0	0	0
Decrypting image	0	0	0	0	0	0	0	0	0	0
Encrypting text	0	0	0	0	0	0	0	0	0	0
Decrypting text	0	0	0	0	0	0	0	0	0	0

The table 2 demonstrates the performance metrics of the RC4 encryption algorithm for both image and text data, recording extraordinarily low times across all trials with every encryption and decryption operation completing in nearly zero microseconds. This level of efficiency, indicated by consistently minimal processing times, underscores RC4's potential for rapid transaction processing within systems that require fast data handling. However, despite this speed, RC4's relatively weaker security features compared to more contemporary encryption algorithms pose significant risks, especially in environments like pharmaceutical supply chains where the protection of sensitive data is paramount. These results illustrate the critical trade-off between RC4's operational speed and its adequacy in ensuring robust data security.

Table 3. DES Encryption and Decryption Performance for Image and text Data in Microseconds

DES (image)	1	2	3	4	5	6	7	8	9	10
Encrypting image	774	590	88	502	609	503	641	585	631	524
Decrypting image	516	643	503	504	608	558	663	506	529	595
Encrypting text	0	0	0	0	0	0	0	0	0	0
Decrypting text	0	0	0	0	0	0	0	0	0	0

The Table 3 showcases the performance of the Data Encryption Standard (DES) for both image and text data, highlighting its efficiency in encryption and decryption processes. Encryption times for images varied, with a range from a low of 88 microseconds to a high of 774 microseconds, demonstrating moderate variability. Similarly, decryption times also showed a moderate spread, from 503 to 663 microseconds. For text data, both encryption and decryption times were consistently zero microseconds across all trials, indicating extremely rapid processing for simpler data types. Despite these relatively quick processing times, DES's known security vulnerabilities could limit its suitability for highly secure applications such as those in pharmaceutical supply chains, where protecting sensitive data against modern threats is crucial. This analysis underlines the need for a careful balance between performance efficiency and security robustness in selecting encryption standards for critical systems.

The Table 4 displays the performance of the ChaCha20 encryption algorithm for both image and text data, illustrating its efficiency and reliability in handling

Table 4. Chacha20 Encryption and Decryption Performance for Image and text Data in Microseconds

CHACHA20 (image)	1	2	3	4	5	6	7	8	9	10
Encrypting image	544	0	0	519	0	0	629	518	149	142
Decrypting image	0	0	1503	0	331	0	0	0	0	0
Encrypting text	0	0	0	0	0	0	0	0	0	0
Decrypting text	0	0	0	0	0	0	0	0	0	0

encryption tasks. For image data, the encryption times show considerable efficiency, ranging from 0 to 629 microseconds, with most values being notably low or zero, highlighting the algorithm's rapid processing capability. The most significant outlier in decryption times for images is 1,503 microseconds in one trial, with all other decryption events for images and all encryption and decryption events for text consistently registering zero microseconds. This performance profile underscores ChaCha20's potential as a highly effective encryption solution, combining quick operational speeds with robust security, making it a compelling choice for securing metadata in environments such as pharmaceutical supply chains where both efficiency and security are critical.

Table 5. Blowfish Encryption and Decryption Performance for Image and text Data in Microseconds

blowfish (image)	1	2	3	4	5	6	7	8	9	10
Encrypting image	504	582	586	545	632	505	688	0	633	541
Decrypting image	0	508	190	0	0	103	0	470	575	532
Encrypting text	0	0	0	0	0	0	91	0	0	0
Decrypting text	0	0	0	0	0	0	0	0	0	0

The Table 5 outlines the performance data for the Blowfish encryption algorithm, used in tests for both image and text data. For image data, the encryption times are mostly moderate, varying from 504 to 688 microseconds, with one instance showing a zero-microsecond result, indicating occasional rapid processing. Decryption times for images exhibit some variability, with several instances at zero microseconds interspersed with times up to 575 microseconds. Notably, encryption and decryption times for text data consistently register at zero microseconds, except for a single 91-microsecond occurrence in text encryption. These results reveal that while Blowfish generally provides satisfactory performance with a reasonable balance between speed and security, the presence of more contemporary algorithms that offer enhanced security features may diminish its attractiveness in scenarios demanding the highest levels of data protection.

The Table 6 demonstrates the AES algorithm's encryption and decryption capabilities for image and text data, showcasing its suitability for pharmaceutical supply chain applications. Encryption times for images ranged from 82

Table 6. AES Encryption and Decryption Performance for Image and text Data in Microseconds

AES (image)	1	2	3	4	5	6	7	8	9	10
Encrypting image	621	807	453	82	109	221	610	541	557	503
Decrypting image	0	0	0	0	0	0	0	0	504	0
Encrypting text	0	0	0	0	0	0	0	0	0	0
Decrypting text	0	0	0	0	0	0	0	0	0	0

to 807 microseconds, with decryption mostly occurring instantaneously, except for one trial at 504 microseconds. Text data encryption and decryption consistently recorded zero microseconds, highlighting AES's rapid processing. Its robust security and high performance make AES ideal for systems employing smart contracts, encrypted NFTs, IPFS, and distributed ledgers, ensuring the integrity and efficiency required in managing sensitive medical data.

The data collected from our study provide essential insights into the suitability of each encryption algorithm for use in a transparent, blockchain-based pharmaceutical supply chain management system. We aim to identify an encryption method that enhances the security of encrypted NFT metadata while aligning with the high-paced nature of pharmaceutical transactions, which require both speed and robust security. Our evaluation stresses the need for a carefully considered choice of encryption technology, one that balances stringent security requirements with the operational demands of our blockchain system. By conducting thorough testing and analysis, we seek to strengthen the integrity of the supply chain, thus building trust and reliability from the initial manufacturer to the end consumer.

5 Evaluation

In our analysis of how blockchain technology can enhance transparency in pharmaceutical supply chains, we have identified four EVM-compatible platforms that are well-suited for our smart contracts: Binance Smart Chain (BSC), Polygon, Fantom, and Celo. These platforms were chosen for their distinct capabilities and their potential to efficiently manage supply chain operations. Our strategy includes not only using blockchain for secure transactions and verification but also incorporating decentralized data storage solutions. In particular, we plan to use encrypted NFTs to authenticate significant events within the supply chain. Additionally, for interacting with the InterPlanetary File System (IPFS), we will employ the Pinata platform, which supports decentralized file management. This approach is intended to enhance the management and transparency of both certification and supply chain information.

5.1 Environment Simulation

This scenario outlines a blockchain network designed specifically for the pharmaceutical supply chain, incorporating encrypted NFTs and IPFS to manage and

Fig. 3. Generated IPFS Hash for Stored NFT Metadata

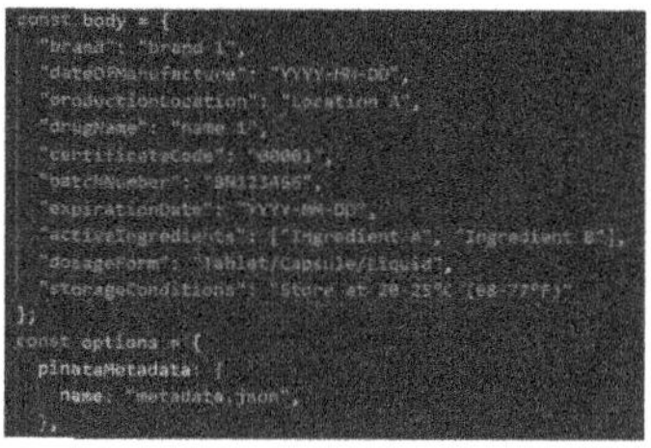

Fig. 4. Defining the Data Structure for Supply Chain Item NFT

verify supply records effectively. Within this network, various supply chain roles such as quality inspectors, manufacturers, and distributors are represented as nodes, each secured using distinct public-private key cryptography. Public keys serve as identifiers for transactions within the network, while private keys ensure the security of these transactions. Tasks performed by these nodes include the creation of encrypted NFTs and the execution of smart contracts. To avoid the typical limitations of resource scarcity, the test environment is equipped with a sufficient supply of ether. This setup allows for a thorough evaluation of how encrypted NFTs and IPFS can be utilized to authenticate and maintain supply chain documentation in a controlled setting, thereby providing insights into the practical use and challenges of this technology for ensuring the integrity of pharmaceutical supply chains without exposing real-world operations to risks.

5.2 Implementing IPFS for Supply Chain Management Systems

To enhance the transparency of the pharmaceutical supply chain, the process of creating an encrypted Non-Fungible Token (NFT) begins by establishing a structured data format for the pharmaceutical product (Fig. 4). This step involves constructing a JSON object that contains essential data points such as the type of drug, its origin, the manufacturing process, and relevant certifications. This JSON object, serving as the metadata for the encrypted NFT, offers a clear record of the pharmaceutical's path through the supply chain. The goal is to provide a level of transparency that fosters trust and clarity among all stakeholders involved.

After setting up the data structure for the encrypted Non-Fungible Token (NFT), the focus turns to verifying the functionality of the associated smart contract (Fig. 5). This crucial verification stage involves rigorous testing to ensure that the smart contract is correctly initiated and operational, effectively managing specified tasks, including those that are time-sensitive. This validation is essential for confirming the reliability of the smart contract in automating encoded processes within the pharmaceutical supply chain. Ensuring that the smart contract functions properly is key to maintaining a transparent and efficient supply chain, leveraging blockchain technology to bolster the management of pharmaceutical logistics.

Following the validation of the smart contract's effectiveness, the next step involves securing the encrypted Non-Fungible Token (NFT) metadata on a decentralized platform to ensure its ongoing preservation and accessibility (Fig. 6). Utilizing Pinata facilitates this process by enabling the efficient upload of metadata JSON files to the InterPlanetary File System (IPFS), thus protecting the digital representation of pharmaceutical supply chain items. Storing the metadata on IPFS, accessible via a unique IPFS hash, creates a durable and retrievable record of the supply chain data. This method supports the transparency and trust in pharmaceutical supply chain management, relying on decentralized storage to maintain a complete and permanent dataset.

The creation of an IPFS hash, as detailed in the documentation, marks a crucial step in associating the encrypted Non-Fungible Token (NFT) with a permanent and unchangeable record of the pharmaceutical supply chain item's metadata (Fig. 3). This hash serves as a unique identifier that ensures the metadata stored on IPFS is preserved intact and accessible to anyone possessing the hash. This phase is essential for linking the NFT to a dependable and immutable record of the supply chain item's details, thereby finalizing the NFT creation process. It underscores the commitment to enhancing the transparency and reliability of pharmaceutical supply chain management by securely storing the supply chain information in a decentralized storage system.

Fig. 5. Test Confirmation of Smart Contract Functionality

Fig. 6. Pinata Cloud Interface for IPFS Metadata Storage

5.3 Testing on EVM-Supported Platforms

Our study employs the Ethereum Virtual Machine (EVM) to implement smart contracts on several EVM-compatible platforms, such as Binance Smart Chain, Polygon, Fantom, and Celo, to analyze their capability in managing a transparent pharmaceutical supply chain. The research focuses on essential functions including data entry for recording supply chain activities, generating encrypted Non-Fungible Tokens (NFTs) for tracking products, and transferring these tokens to secure data sharing across the supply chain. We evaluated each platform based on factors like transaction speed, resource efficiency, and the user-friendliness of their interfaces, which are crucial for their acceptance among supply chain participants. The aim of this evaluation is to determine which platforms most effectively support a transparent and efficient supply chain, particularly in the secure creation and management of encrypted NFTs within the pharmaceutical industry.

Transaction Fee. The table provided offers a detailed comparison of transaction costs on different blockchain platforms, assessing their impact on the overall expenses associated with supply chain management. These transaction fees are vital for determining the operational costs of a blockchain system and are key to evaluating its economic viability. Additionally, the table includes updated information on the token prices for these platforms as of March 27, 2024, at 7:00 AM UTC. This data helps paint a clear picture of the financial landscape of these blockchain networks, supporting the analysis of their appropriateness for a pharmaceutical supply chain integrity system that utilizes Smart Contracts, encrypted Non-Fungible Tokens (NFTs), IPFS, and Distributed Ledgers (Table 7).

Table 7. Transaction fee

	Transaction Creation	Create NFT	Transfer NFT
BNB Smart Chain	0.0273134 BNB ($8.27)	0.00109162 BNB ($0.33)	0.00057003 BNB ($0.17)
Fantom	0.00957754 FTM ($0.00)	0.000405167 FTM ($0.00)	0.0002380105 FTM ($0.00)
Polygon	0.006840710032835408 MATIC ($0.01)	0.000289405001852192 MATIC ($0.00)	0.000170007501088048 MATIC ($0.00)
Celo	0.007097844 CELO ($0.005)	0.0002840812 CELO ($0.000)	0.0001554878 CELO ($0.000)

On the Binance Smart Chain (BSC), recording a new supply chain event, such as the receipt of pharmaceutical ingredients at a facility, incurs a cost of 0.0273134 BNB, or approximately $8.27. This transaction fee applies to typical supply chain activities like documenting arrivals. Additionally, the cost to mint an encrypted Non-Fungible Token (NFT) on BSC, which serves as a digital representation of a physical item or certificate within the supply chain, is 0.00109162 BNB, equivalent to $0.33. This fee covers the creation of a unique token detailing specifics such as the product's origin and certification. Transferring an encrypted NFT within the BSC network, which may involve changing its custody or ownership, is charged at 0.00057003 BNB or $0.17, highlighting the platform's capability for efficient asset transfers.

The Fantom network offers a very low fee structure, with transaction costs for initiating a blockchain entry, creating an encrypted NFT, and transferring an encrypted NFT priced at 0.00957754 FTM, 0.000405167 FTM, and 0.0002380105 FTM, respectively. These fees convert to minimal dollar amounts, making Fantom an economical choice for operations such as tracking pharmaceutical shipments or exchanging important documentation within the supply chain.

Polygon is also known for its cost-effectiveness, with fees for recording an entry, minting an encrypted NFT, and transferring an encrypted NFT set at 0.006840710032835408 MATIC, 0.000289405001852192 MATIC, and 0.000170007501088048 MATIC, respectively. The low costs associated with these actions make Polygon a practical platform for conducting multiple transactions within the pharmaceutical supply chain without substantial financial impact.

Lastly, Celo's fee structure is conducive to economical operations, with charges for making new entries, minting encrypted NFTs, and transferring encrypted NFTs at 0.007097844 CELO, 0.0002840812 CELO, and 0.0001554878 CELO, respectively. These rates, which amount to fractions of a cent, highlight Celo's ability to support high-volume transactions typical of supply chain activities at minimal expense, underscoring its suitability for handling pharmaceutical supply chain management tasks that involve Smart Contracts, encrypted NFTs, IPFS, and Distributed Ledgers.

6 Discussion

6.1 Threats to Validity

One primary threat to the validity of our findings involves the variability of blockchain performance under different network conditions. The transaction speeds and costs reported may fluctuate based on network congestion, changes in token value, and updates to platform algorithms, which were not accounted for in this static evaluation. Additionally, our analysis assumes that the blockchain's security features, such as encryption and decentralized storage, function flawlessly. Any vulnerabilities in these features or in the underlying blockchain protocol could compromise the results and effectiveness of the supply chain solutions discussed.

6.2 Limitations

The study is limited by its focus on only a select few blockchain platforms, which may not represent the broader spectrum of available technologies that could potentially be adapted for pharmaceutical supply chains. Furthermore, the assessment predominantly relies on quantitative metrics such as transaction costs and speeds, potentially overlooking qualitative aspects like user experience, interoperability between different blockchain systems, and the ease of integrating these platforms with existing pharmaceutical logistics infrastructures.

6.3 Future Work

Future research should aim to address these limitations by including a wider range of blockchain platforms and by exploring additional factors that affect their practicality for pharmaceutical supply chains. It would be beneficial to conduct dynamic tests that simulate real-world conditions more closely, such as varying network loads and potential security threats, to evaluate the robustness of each platform. Moreover, future studies could develop more comprehensive criteria that include qualitative evaluations of platform usability and integration capabilities. Investigating the long-term sustainability of implementing blockchain solutions in pharmaceutical supply chains and their acceptance among various stakeholders will also be crucial. Further research could explore the development of standardized protocols to enhance interoperability between different blockchain systems, which would help streamline processes across diverse supply chain segments.

7 Conclusion

This study has introduced and assessed a blockchain-based framework designed to enhance the integrity of pharmaceutical supply chains. By integrating smart contracts, encrypted NFTs, IPFS, and distributed ledger technologies, we have developed a system that significantly improves transparency and ensures data integrity throughout the supply chain. The use of various encryption algorithms was scrutinized to find the most effective balance between security and operational efficiency, with our findings favoring a tailored approach to encryption based on the specific needs of the pharmaceutical sector. The evaluation conducted on multiple EVM-compatible platforms demonstrated the system's flexibility and effectiveness, showing promising results in terms of speed, efficiency, and cost-effectiveness. The model established through this research addresses key issues such as ethical sourcing, transparency, and efficiency, thereby providing a viable solution to the longstanding challenges faced by the pharmaceutical industry. Ultimately, our work underscores the potential of blockchain technology to create a more secure, transparent, and fair pharmaceutical supply chain, encouraging further research and adoption of these technologies within the industry.

References

1. Ali, S., et al.: Tracing pharmaceutical products utilizing blockchain technologies. Int. J. Comput. Digit. Syst. **12**, 1173–1181 (2022)
2. A.A.B. Amarasinghe, G., et al.: SUPPLYDECK - a blockchain-based pharmaceutical supply chain management. In: 2022 4th International Conference on Advancements in Computing (ICAC) (2022)
3. Bali, V., et al.: Combating drug counterfeiting by tracing ownership transfer using blockchain technology. J. Pharm. Secur. **13**, 1–21 (2022)
4. Botcha, K.M., Chakravarthy, V.V., Anurag: Enhancing traceability in pharmaceutical supply chain using internet of things (IoT) and blockchain (2019)
5. Dave, M., et al.: Monitoring supply chain of pharmaceutical drugs using blockchain (2022)
6. Duong-Trung, N., et al.: Multi-sessions mechanism for decentralized cash on delivery system. Int. J. Adv. Comput. Sci. Appl **10**(9) (2019)
7. Gebreab, S.A., et al.: NFT-based traceability and ownership management of medical devices. IEEE Access **10**, 126394–126411 (2022)

8. Ha, X.S., et al.: DeM-CoD: novel access-control-based cash on delivery mechanism for decentralized marketplace. In: 2020 IEEE 19th International Conference on Trust, Security and Privacy in Computing and Communications (TrustCom), pp. 71–78. IEEE (2020)
9. Ha, X.S., Le, T.H., Phan, T.T., Nguyen, H.H.D., Vo, H.K., Duong-Trung, N.: Scrutinizing trust and transparency in cash on delivery systems. In: Wang, G., Chen, B., Li, W., Di Pietro, R., Yan, X., Han, H. (eds.) SpaCCS 2020. LNCS, vol. 12382, pp. 214–227. Springer, Cham (2021). https://doi.org/10.1007/978-3-030-68851-6_15
10. Haq, I., Esuka, O.M..: Blockchain technology in pharmaceutical industry to prevent counterfeit drugs. J. Pharm. Innov. **25**, 8–12 (2018)
11. Hawashin, D., et al.: Using composable NFTs for trading and managing expensive packaged products in the food industry. IEEE Access **11**, 10587–10603 (2023)
12. Kumar, R. and Tripathi, R.: Traceability of counterfeit medicine supply chain through blockchain. Int. J. Drug Safety (2019)
13. Kumar, M.M., Kumar, M.L., Jai, M., Sharma, M.Y.: MedBust: blockchain in pharmaceutical supply chain. Pharm. Supply Chain Manag. Rev. **1**, 2Professor(2023)
14. Le, H.T., et al.: Introducing multi shippers mechanism for decentralized cash on delivery system. Int. J. Adv. Comput. Sci. Appl. **10**(6) (2019)
15. Le, N.T.T., et al.: Assuring non-fraudulent transactions in cash on delivery by introducing double smart contracts. Int. J. Adv. Comput. Sci. Appl. **10**(5), 677–684 (2019)
16. Lingayat, A., et al.: Securing pharmaceutical supply chain using blockchain technology (2021)
17. Musamih, A., et al.: A blockchain-based approach for drug traceability in healthcare supply chain (2023)
18. Nawale, S.D., Konapure, R.R.: Blockchain & IoT based drugs traceability for pharma industry (2021)
19. Pathak, A., et al.: Blockchain technology in pharmaceutical supply chain management. J. Pharm. Supply Chain Manag. (2022)
20. Pawar, M.K., Patil, P., Sharma, M., Chalageri, M.: Secure and scalable decentralized supply chain management using Ethereum and IPFS platform. In: 2021 International Conference on Intelligent Technologies (CONIT), pp. 1–5. IEEE (2021)
21. Rai, A., Srivastava, S., Arora, A.: Blockchain-based traceability of counterfeited drugs (2023)
22. Rai, B.K. BBTCD: blockchain based traceability of counterfeited drugs. Health Serv. Outcomes Res. Method **23**, 337–353 (2023). https://doi.org/10.1007/s10742-022-00292-w
23. Rayan, R.A., Zubair, M.A.M.: IoT-integrated blockchain in the drug supply chain (2021). https://doi.org/10.1007/978-3-030-65691-1_7
24. Shalini, S., et al.: An effective counterfeit medicine authentication system using blockchain and IoT (2023)
25. Saindane, P., et al.: Blockchain: a solution for improved traceability with reduced counterfeits in supply chain of drugs (2020)
26. Singh, R., Dwivedi, A.D., Srivastava, G.: Internet of things based blockchain for temperature monitoring and counterfeit pharmaceutical prevention. Sensors **20**, 3951 (2020)
27. Uddin, M.: Blockchain medledger: a hyperledger fabric enabled drug traceability system for counterfeit drugs in pharmaceutical industry. Int. J. Pharm. **597**, 120235 (2021)

Comparative Analysis of EVM-Supported Blockchain Platforms for Enhancing Organ Donation Supply Chain Management

Loc V. C. P.[1], Khanh V. H.[1], Ngan N. T. K.[2(✉)], Khoa T. D.[1], Triet N. M.[1], Khiem H. G.[1], Nam T. B.[1], and Anh N. T.[1]

[1] FPT University, Can Tho, Vietnam
locvcpce160307@fpt.edu.vn
[2] FPT Polytecnic, Can Tho, Vietnam
nganntkpc06789@fpt.edu.vn

Abstract. This study examines the potential of blockchain technology to address challenges in organ donation supply chain management. Traditional centralized systems face limitations in transparency, efficiency, and scalability. We evaluate four Ethereum Virtual Machine (EVM)-supported platforms-Binance Smart Chain, Fantom, Polygon, and Celo-for their suitability in improving organ donation processes. The research focuses on transaction efficiency, cost-effectiveness, scalability, and accessibility. We also explore the integration of Non-Fungible Tokens (NFTs) for secure data management. Our comparative analysis aims to identify optimal blockchain solutions for enhancing transparency, efficiency, and trust in organ donation systems. The findings contribute to the ongoing efforts to improve organ transplantation outcomes and may inform future implementations of blockchain technology in healthcare supply chain management.

Keywords: Organ donation · Blockchain · EVM platforms · NFT · Healthcare systems

1 Introduction

Organ donation management is a critical component of healthcare systems worldwide, traditionally relying on centralized databases overseen by government or healthcare organizations [3,4]. These systems store and manage detailed information about donors and recipients, with healthcare professionals playing a pivotal role in maintaining records and coordinating with hospitals and organ procurement organizations for organ matching and transplantation processes (e.g., blood donation [9,17]). While these systems have been instrumental in saving lives, they face several challenges that limit their effectiveness and efficiency. The conventional approach to organ donation management, largely dependent on manual processes and subjective decision-making, has raised concerns about

S. He and L.-J. Zhang (Eds.): SCF/SCC 2024, LNCS 15430, pp. 33–46, 2025.
https://doi.org/10.1007/978-3-031-77000-5_3

transparency, efficiency, and scalability [14]. These issues have led to a growing interest in exploring alternative solutions that can address these limitations and improve the overall organ donation process [2].

Blockchain technology has emerged as a potential solution to enhance the organ donation supply chain [1]. By leveraging its decentralized and transparent nature, blockchain offers the possibility of creating a more efficient, secure, and trustworthy system for managing organ donations [11]. The integration of blockchain technology with Non-Fungible Tokens (NFTs) and various Ethereum Virtual Machine (EVM)-supported platforms presents an opportunity to revolutionize the organ donation management landscape [6]. This study focuses on evaluating the potential of blockchain technology in organ donation management across four EVM-supported platforms: Binance Smart Chain (BNB), Fantom, Polygon, and Celo. Each of these platforms offers unique features that could potentially address different aspects of the organ donation process. The use of NFTs in this context provides a secure method for storing and managing critical organ donation data, ensuring unique identification and maintaining data integrity throughout the donation lifecycle.

The analysis of these platforms aims to assess their suitability for handling various aspects of the organ donation process, including transaction efficiency, cost-effectiveness, scalability, and accessibility. By examining the performance of these platforms in managing high-volume transactions, supporting complex operations, and providing mobile accessibility, this study seeks to identify the most suitable blockchain solutions for enhancing the organ donation supply chain. Through this comparative analysis, we aim to contribute to the ongoing efforts to improve organ donation management systems. By leveraging the strengths of blockchain technology and the specific features of different EVM-supported platforms, there is potential to create a more transparent, efficient, and reliable organ donation process. This approach could not only address the limitations of traditional systems but also foster greater trust among donors, recipients, and healthcare providers, ultimately leading to improved outcomes in organ transplantation.

2 Prior Work

Recent research has explored the application of blockchain technology to address challenges in organ donation and transplantation processes. Studies have focused on developing systems that enhance transparency, security, and efficiency in the organ donation supply chain. Several researchers have proposed blockchain-based solutions for managing organ donation. These systems aim to improve fairness, efficiency, and patient trust through secure, traceable, and auditable smart contracts [6]. The integration of electronic medical records with decentralized storage has been suggested to enhance data consistency and reliability [22]. Some studies have also explored the potential of combining artificial intelligence with blockchain technology in this domain [12].

The use of blockchain for secure, decentralized management of organ donation has been advocated to address existing challenges in the field [21]. Researchers have designed scalable blockchain platforms that automate organ donation processes using smart contracts [15]. The importance of monitoring and transparency, particularly in kidney donations, has led to proposals integrating Internet of Things (IoT) devices with blockchain for improved management [10]. Ethical concerns regarding organ distribution and black market activities have been highlighted, emphasizing the need for more organized approaches [1]. To address these issues, blockchain-based systems have been proposed to combat organ trafficking through enhanced traceability and accountability [20]. Recent advancements have also explored the integration of Non-Fungible Tokens (NFTs) and the InterPlanetary File System (IPFS) in organ donation management. These technologies offer potential solutions for donor-recipient matching, real-time organ tracking, and donation incentivization [5]. The use of NFTs in healthcare presents a new approach to handling medical data and patient records, focusing on data privacy and ownership [18].

Blockchain-based management systems for both blood and organ donations have been developed, offering decentralized platforms that aim to improve upon traditional centralized systems [6,7]. These systems often utilize smart contracts for automating matching processes and IPFS for secure data storage, addressing challenges related to transparency and mismanagement [16]. The potential of blockchain technology in organ donation extends to cost reduction by eliminating third-party intermediaries in organ and tissue transplantation processes [19]. These developments suggest a possible transformation in healthcare, particularly in streamlining organ donation systems and promoting trust among participants [8,13].

Overall, the application of blockchain technology in the organ donation supply chain shows potential for addressing longstanding challenges in the field. However, further research and practical implementations are needed to fully realize these benefits and overcome existing limitations.

3 Methodology

3.1 Traditional Model for Organ Distribution Process

Figure 1 illustrates the comprehensive process of organ donation, from initial registration to final distribution among medical centers. This workflow begins with organ donors, who take the first step by completing an organ registration form. This form serves as a formal declaration of their intent to donate and captures essential information about the potential donor. Once the registration is complete, the process moves to the organ receiving center. This facility plays a pivotal role in the organ donation ecosystem, acting as a central hub for coordinating various aspects of the donation process. The receiving center is responsible for multiple critical functions, including the initial assessment of donated organs, matching them with compatible recipients, and overseeing the logistical challenges of organ preservation and transportation. An interesting aspect of this process is the issuance of an organ certificate by the receiving center. This document likely serves as an official record of the donation, potentially including details about the organ's condition, donor information (while

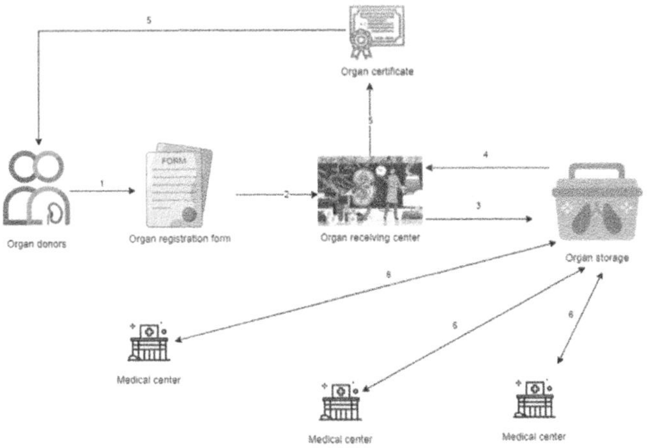

Fig. 1. Organ Donation and Distribution Process

maintaining appropriate privacy), and other relevant data that may be crucial for medical professionals involved in the transplantation process. The certificate adds a layer of documentation and accountability to the system, ensuring that all parties involved have access to necessary information.

The diagram also highlights the importance of organ storage facilities in this process. These specialized units are designed to preserve organs in optimal conditions, maintaining their viability for transplantation. The storage phase is critical, as it provides a buffer between the time an organ becomes available and when it can be transplanted into a recipient. This storage capability allows for more flexibility in matching donors to recipients and can potentially increase the number of successful transplants. The final stage of the process involves the distribution of organs to various medical centers. This step underscores the collaborative nature of organ donation systems, where multiple hospitals and medical facilities work together to ensure that organs reach the patients who need them most urgently. The bidirectional arrows between the organ storage and medical centers suggest a dynamic system where organs may be redistributed as needed, optimizing the use of this precious resource and maximizing the potential to save lives through transplantation.

3.2 Blockchain-Based Organ Donation Distributed System

Figure 2 presents a comprehensive overview of an organ donation management system that incorporates various technological elements to streamline the process from donation to transplantation. This system appears to integrate traditional medical procedures with digital technologies, creating a more efficient and transparent workflow for organ donation and distribution. At the core of this system is a user interface (UI/UX) component, which serves as the central hub for information exchange and process management. This interface likely provides access

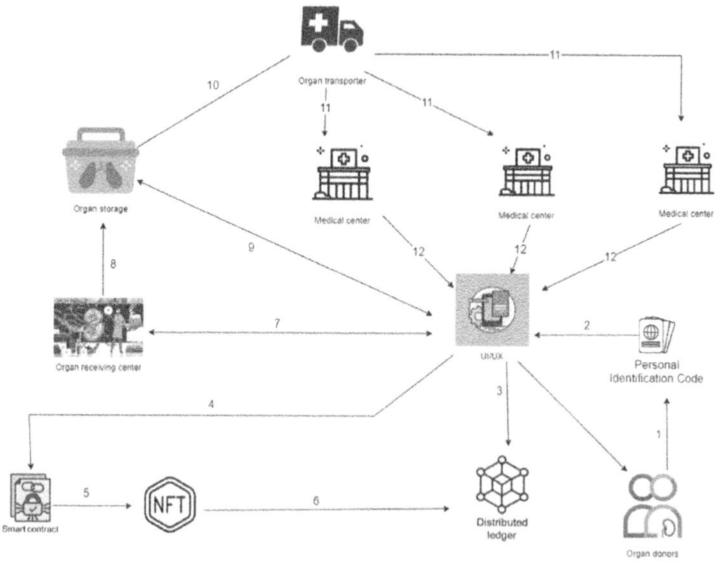

Fig. 2. Blockchain-based Organ Donation and Distribution System

points for different stakeholders involved in the organ donation process, including donors, medical professionals, and administrators. The UI/UX component interacts with several other elements of the system, facilitating communication and data flow between various stages of the organ donation process.

The system employs blockchain technology, as evidenced by the inclusion of a distributed ledger and smart contracts. These technologies can enhance the security and traceability of organ donation records. Smart contracts, in particular, could automate certain aspects of the donation process, ensuring that predefined conditions are met before proceeding to subsequent stages. The use of Non-Fungible Tokens (NFTs) in conjunction with smart contracts suggests a method for uniquely identifying and tracking individual organ donations throughout the process. The diagram also illustrates the physical components of the organ donation system, including organ storage facilities, medical centers, and transportation services. These elements are crucial for the practical aspects of organ preservation and distribution. The organ transporter, represented by an ambulance icon, indicates the critical role of timely and specialized transportation in the organ donation process. The connection between the organ storage and the UI/UX component suggests that the system tracks the status and location of organs in real-time, potentially optimizing allocation and reducing waste. Personal Identification Codes for organ donors are included in the system, highlighting the importance of donor privacy and consent management. The organ receiving center plays a pivotal role, interfacing with both the digital components of the system and the physical storage and transportation elements. This integration of digital and physical processes demonstrates an attempt to create a holistic approach to organ donation management, potentially improving efficiency and reducing the risk of errors or delays in this time-sensitive field.

4 Evaluation

In the evaluation section of our study on blockchain-based organ donation systems, we focus on cross-chain analysis, examining four EVM-supported platforms: *Binance Smart Chain (BNB Smart Chain)*[1], *Polygon*[2], *Fantom*[3], and *Celo*[4]. The rationale behind considering multiple platforms stems from the understanding that each blockchain network possesses unique characteristics that can significantly impact the performance, cost-effectiveness, and overall suitability for organ donation management. By evaluating several platforms, we aim to identify the most appropriate option that balances various factors critical to the organ donation process. Each blockchain network offers different trade-offs in terms of transaction speed, cost, and scalability, which are crucial considerations in the time-sensitive and resource-intensive field of organ donation. Furthermore, the diverse nature of these platforms allows us to assess how different consensus mechanisms, network architectures, and economic models affect the implementation of organ donation management systems.

To conduct a comprehensive assessment, we analyze three primary methods essential to the organ donation process: transaction creation, NFT minting, and NFT transfer. Transaction creation represents the foundational operation of recording donation information on the blockchain. NFT minting is crucial for creating unique digital representations of each organ, ensuring traceability and preventing duplication. NFT transfer simulates the movement of organs through various stages of the donation and transplantation process, from donor to recipient.

Our analysis encompasses several key metrics that provide insight into the performance and economic aspects of each platform. We examine the transaction fee, which represents the cost associated with executing operations on the blockchain. This fee is a critical factor in determining the economic viability of implementing a blockchain-based organ donation system. We also consider the burn fee, which some platforms implement as a deflationary mechanism, potentially affecting the long-term cost structure of the system. Gas limit and gas used by transactions are analyzed to understand the computational resources required for different operations across platforms. These metrics help in assessing the efficiency and scalability of each network in handling organ donation-related transactions. Additionally, we evaluate the gas price, which fluctuates based on network congestion and demand, to gauge the potential variability in transaction costs over time. By examining these factors across multiple platforms, we aim to provide a nuanced understanding of how different blockchain networks perform

[1] https://github.com/bnb-chain/whitepaper/blob/master/WHITEPAPER.md.
[2] https://polygon.technology/lightpaper-polygon.pdf.
[3] https://whitepaper.io/document/438/fantom-whitepaper.
[4] https://celo.org/papers/whitepaper.

in the context of organ donation management. This comparative analysis will help identify the platform that offers the best combination of performance, cost-effectiveness, and reliability for implementing a blockchain-based organ donation system.

4.1 Transaction Fee

Table 1. Transaction fee

	Contracts Creation	Create NFT	Transfer NFT
BNB Smart Chain	0.02731184 BNB ($16.02)	0.00109162 BNB ($0.64)	0.00057003 BNB ($0.33)
Fantom	0.009576994 FTM ($0.001)	0.000405167 FTM ($0.000)	0.0002380105 FTM ($0.000)
Polygon	0.006840710032835408 MATIC($0.000)	0.000289405001852192 MATIC($0.000)	0.000170007501088048 MATIC($0.00)
Celo	0.0070974384 CELO ($0.000)	0.0002840812 CELO ($0.000)	0.0001554878 CELO ($0.000)

The analysis of transaction fees across the four EVM-supported platforms is presented in Table 1. BNB Smart Chain demonstrates the highest transaction fees among the platforms examined. For contract creation, BNB Smart Chain incurs a fee of 0.02731184 BNB, equivalent to approximately $16.02. This cost is notably higher compared to the other platforms, potentially due to BNB's higher market value and network demand. The fees for creating and transferring NFTs on BNB Smart Chain are comparatively lower at 0.00109162 BNB ($0.64) and 0.00057003 BNB ($0.33) respectively, yet still exceed those of the other platforms. In contrast, Fantom, Polygon, and Celo exhibit substantially lower transaction fees across all operations. Fantom's fees range from 0.009576994 FTM ($0.001) for contract creation to 0.0002380105 FTM ($0.000) for NFT transfer. Polygon shows even lower fees, with contract creation costing 0.006840710032835408 MATIC ($0.000) and NFT transfer at 0.000170007501088048 MATIC ($0.00). Celo's fee structure is similar to Fantom and Polygon, with contract creation at 0.0070974384 CELO ($0.000) and NFT transfer at 0.0001554878 CELO ($0.000).

The stark difference in transaction fees between BNB Smart Chain and the other platforms warrants consideration in the context of organ donation systems. While BNB Smart Chain may offer advantages in terms of ecosystem support and liquidity, the higher transaction costs could potentially impact the scalability and cost-effectiveness of organ donation management, especially for high-volume operations. Conversely, the negligible fees on Fantom, Polygon, and Celo suggest these platforms might be more suitable for frequent, small-scale transactions typical in organ donation tracking and management. It is important to note that while the fees for Fantom, Polygon, and Celo appear minimal in USD terms, the actual cost in native tokens should not be overlooked. These fees, though small, still represent a real cost in the respective ecosystems and could accumulate over time with high transaction volumes. Additionally, the fee structures observed here may fluctuate based on network congestion and token value, factors that should be considered in long-term planning for blockchain-based organ donation systems.

4.2 Burn Fee

Table 2. Burn fee

	Contracts Creation	Create NFT	Transfer NFT
BNB Smart Chain	0.002731184 BNB ($1.6)	0.000109162 BNB ($0.06)	0.000057003 BNB ($0.03)
Fantom	do not mention	do not mention	do not mention
Polygon	0.{10}032835408 MATIC ($0.00)	0.1101852192 MATIC($0.00)	0.{11}01088048 MATIC($0.00)
Celo	do not mention	do not mention	do not mention

The analysis of burn fees across the four EVM-supported platforms reveals interesting variations in their tokenomics and fee structures. Burn fees, Table 2, which involve permanently removing a portion of tokens from circulation, can play a significant role in the long-term economics of blockchain networks and, by extension, the cost dynamics of organ donation management systems implemented on these platforms. BNB Smart Chain implements a burn fee mechanism across all three examined operations. For contract creation, the burn fee is 0.002731184 BNB, equivalent to approximately $1.6. This represents a notable cost, especially for operations that might need to be performed frequently in an organ donation management system. The burn fees for creating and transferring NFTs on BNB Smart Chain are lower at 0.000109162 BNB ($0.06) and 0.000057003 BNB ($0.03) respectively, but still constitute a tangible cost. Polygon also incorporates a burn fee mechanism, albeit with much lower values compared to BNB Smart Chain. The burn fees on Polygon are fractions of a MATIC token, with contract creation incurring a burn fee of 0.{10}032835408 MATIC, NFT creation 0.{11}01852192 MATIC, and NFT transfer 0.{11}01088048 MATIC. While these amounts translate to nearly $0.00 in current USD terms, they still represent a deflationary mechanism within the Polygon ecosystem.

Interestingly, Fantom and Celo do not implement burn fees for the operations examined in this study. This absence of burn fees could potentially lead to lower overall transaction costs on these platforms, which might be advantageous for high-frequency, low-value transactions typical in organ donation tracking systems. The presence or absence of burn fees, and their relative magnitudes, can have implications for the long-term sustainability and cost structure of blockchain-based organ donation systems. Platforms with burn fees may offer increased scarcity of their native tokens over time, potentially affecting transaction costs. Conversely, platforms without burn fees might maintain more stable transaction costs but could face different economic challenges in the long run. These factors should be carefully considered when selecting a platform for implementing organ donation management systems, particularly when projecting long-term operational costs and system scalability (Table 3).

4.3 Gas Limit

Table 3. Gas limit

	Contracts Creation	Create NFT	Transfer NFT
BNB Smart Chain	2,731,184	109,162	3,000,000
Fantom	2,736,284	115,762	72,803
Polygon	2,736,284	115,762	72,803
Celo	3,548,719	142,040	85,673

The analysis of gas limits across the four EVM-supported platforms provides insight into the computational resources allocated for different operations in blockchain-based organ donation management systems. Table 4 represent the maximum amount of computational work that can be performed in a single transaction, directly impacting the complexity and scale of operations that can be executed. For contract creation, we observe relatively consistent gas limits across BNB Smart Chain, Fantom, and Polygon, with values of 2,731,184, 2,736,284, and 2,736,284 respectively. This similarity suggests a standard approach to complex operations like deploying smart contracts across these platforms. Celo, however, stands out with a notably higher gas limit of 3,548,719 for contract creation, potentially allowing for more complex or feature-rich smart contracts to be deployed in a single transaction.

In the case of NFT creation, we see more variation. BNB Smart Chain has the lowest gas limit at 109,162, while Fantom and Polygon share an identical limit of 115,762. Celo again offers the highest gas limit at 142,040. These differences could impact the complexity of NFT metadata or additional functions that can be included during the minting process, which may be relevant for capturing detailed information about donated organs. For NFT transfers, an operation likely to be frequent in organ donation tracking, we observe significant disparities. BNB Smart Chain has an unusually high gas limit of 3,000,000, which seems disproportionate compared to the other platforms and the complexity of the operation. Fantom and Polygon share a more modest gas limit of 72,803, while Celo allows for slightly more computational work with a limit of 85,673.

These variations in gas limits across platforms and operations have implications for the design and implementation of organ donation management systems. Higher gas limits, as seen in Celo for most operations, could allow for more complex operations or richer data structures in a single transaction. However, this potential advantage should be weighed against other factors such as transaction speed and cost. The exceptionally high gas limit for NFT transfers on BNB

Smart Chain might offer flexibility but could also lead to inefficiencies if not fully utilized. Platforms with lower gas limits might necessitate more careful optimization of smart contract code and data structures to ensure all necessary operations can be performed within the given constraints.

4.4 Gas Used by Transaction

Table 4. Gas Used by Transaction

	Contracts Creation	Create NFT	Transfer NFT
BNB Smart Chain	2,731,184 (100%)	109,162 (100%)	57,003 (1.9%)
Fantom	2,736,284 (100%)	115,762 (100%)	68,003 (93.41%)
Polygon	2,736,284 (100%)	115,762 (100%)	68,003 (93.41%)
Celo	2,729,784 (76.92%)	109,262 (76.92%)	59,803 (69.8%)

This metric reflects the actual computational resources consumed by each operation, which directly impacts transaction costs and network congestion - Table 4. For contract creation, we observe that BNB Smart Chain, Fantom, and Polygon utilize 100% of their respective gas limits. This full utilization suggests that these platforms have optimized their gas limits to closely match the computational requirements of contract deployment. Celo, however, uses 2,729,784 gas units, which is 76.92% of its higher gas limit. This lower percentage utilization on Celo could indicate either more efficient contract deployment or an overestimation of the required gas limit. In the case of NFT creation, a similar pattern emerges. BNB Smart Chain, Fantom, and Polygon again use 100% of their allocated gas limits, while Celo uses 109,262 gas units, representing 76.92% of its limit. This consistency in utilization percentages across different operations on Celo suggests a systematic approach to gas limit setting on this platform, potentially providing a buffer for more complex operations. The most notable variations are observed in NFT transfers. BNB Smart Chain stands out with a remarkably low gas usage of 57,003 units, merely 1.9% of its unusually high gas limit for this operation. This stark underutilization could indicate an opportunity for gas limit optimization on BNB Smart Chain for NFT transfers. Fantom and Polygon demonstrate high efficiency, using 68,003 gas units, which is 93.41% of their gas limit. Celo uses 59,803 gas units, 69.8% of its limit, maintaining its trend of lower percentage utilization compared to its gas limit.

These variations in gas usage have important implications for the implementation of organ donation management systems. The high utilization rates seen in contract creation and NFT minting across all platforms suggest that these operations are well-optimized and predictable in their resource consumption. However, the significant differences in NFT transfer efficiency, particularly on BNB Smart Chain, highlight the importance of platform-specific optimization for frequent operations in organ tracking systems. The consistent underutilization on Celo across all operations could provide a safety margin for more complex transactions, potentially allowing for additional data or functionality to be included without hitting gas limits. However, this should be balanced against potential inefficiencies in gas price calculations. For high-frequency operations like NFT transfers in organ tracking, the high efficiency demonstrated by Fantom and Polygon could translate to more predictable and potentially lower transaction costs.

4.5 Gas Price

Table 5. Gas Price

	Contracts Creation	Create NFT	Transfer NFT
BNB Smart Chain	0.00000001 BNB (10 Gwei)	0.00000001 BNB (10 Gwei)	0.00000001 BNB (10 Gwei)
Fantom	0.0000000035 FTM (3.5 Gwei)	0.0000000035 FTM (3.5 Gwei)	0.0000000035 FTM (3.5 Gwei)
Polygon	0.000000002500000012 MATIC (2.500000012 Gwei)	0.000000002500000016 MATIC (2.500000016 Gwei)	0.000000002500000016 MATIC (2.500000016 Gwei)
Celo	0.0000000026 CELO (Max Fee per Gas: 2.7 Gwei)	0.0000000026 CELO (Max Fee per Gas: 2.7 Gwei)	0.0000000026 CELO (Max Fee per Gas: 2.7 Gwei)

The analysis of gas prices across the four EVM-supported platforms is provided in Table 5. Gas prices, typically measured in Gwei (10^{-9} of the native token), directly influence the overall transaction costs and can significantly impact the economic viability of implementing such systems on different platforms.

BNB Smart Chain demonstrates a consistent gas price of 0.00000001 BNB (10 Gwei) across all three operations examined: contract creation, NFT creation, and NFT transfer. This uniformity simplifies cost predictions for different types of transactions but also means that all operations, regardless of complexity, incur the same base cost per unit of gas. At 10 Gwei, BNB Smart Chain's gas price is the highest among the platforms studied, which could lead to higher overall transaction costs, especially for gas-intensive operations like contract deployment. Fantom operates with a lower and equally consistent gas price of 0.0000000035 FTM (3.5 Gwei) across all operations. This lower gas price could translate to more cost-effective transactions, particularly for frequent operations like NFT transfers in an organ tracking system. The consistency across operation types, similar to BNB Smart Chain, offers predictability in transaction costs.

Polygon presents a slightly more complex pricing structure. While the gas price is consistent at approximately 2.5 Gwei for NFT creation and transfer, there's a minute variation for contract creation (2.500000012 Gwei vs. 2.500000016 Gwei). This difference, though extremely small, hints at a more dynamic gas pricing mechanism. Polygon's gas prices are the lowest among the platforms examined, potentially offering the most cost-effective solution for high-frequency transactions. Celo utilizes a different approach, specifying a maximum fee per gas of 2.7

Gwei (0.0000000026 CELO) across all operations. This 'max fee' model suggests that actual transaction costs might be lower depending on network conditions, providing potential cost savings. Celo's gas pricing falls between Fantom and Polygon, offering a balance of cost-effectiveness and network security.

These variations in gas prices have significant implications for the implementation of organ donation management systems. BNB Smart Chain's higher gas prices might result in higher overall costs, especially for complex or frequent operations. Conversely, Polygon's lower gas prices could make it more suitable for systems requiring numerous transactions. Fantom and Celo offer middle-ground options, with Celo's max fee model potentially providing additional cost optimization opportunities. It's important to note that while gas prices are a crucial factor, they should be considered alongside other metrics like transaction speed, network congestion, and overall platform stability when choosing a blockchain for organ donation management. Additionally, gas prices can fluctuate based on network demand, so long-term cost projections should account for potential variability in these prices.

5 Conclusion

Our comparative analysis of EVM-supported blockchain platforms reveals promising avenues for enhancing organ donation supply chain management. Each platform-Binance Smart Chain, Fantom, Polygon, and Celo-offers unique strengths that address various aspects of the organ donation process. The integration of NFTs provides a secure method for managing critical donation data, ensuring integrity throughout the donation lifecycle. The study highlights the potential of blockchain technology to significantly improve transparency, efficiency, and trust in organ donation systems. By leveraging decentralized ledgers and smart contracts, these platforms can automate processes, reduce human error, and provide a more equitable organ allocation system. The enhanced traceability and security offered by blockchain technology also address concerns related to data silos and system integrity. However, challenges remain in the widespread adoption of blockchain technology in healthcare settings. These include regulatory hurdles, integration with existing healthcare IT infrastructure, and ensuring patient data privacy. Future research should focus on addressing these challenges and conducting real-world pilot studies to validate the effectiveness of blockchain-based organ donation management systems.

References

1. Chaudhary, N., Manvi, S.S., Koul, N.: Organ bank based on blockchain. In: 2022 IEEE International Conference on Electronics, Computing and Communication Technologies (CONECCT), pp. 1–5. IEEE (2022)
2. DePalma, J.A., Townsend, R.: Ethical issues in organ donation and transplantation: are we helping a few at the expense of many? Crit. Care Nurs. Q. **19**(1), 1–9 (1996)

3. Duong-Trung, N., et al.: On components of a patient-centered healthcare system using smart contract. In: Proceedings of the 2020 4th International Conference on Cryptography, Security and Privacy, pp. 31–35 (2020)
4. Duong-Trung, N., et al.: Smart care: integrating blockchain technology into the design of patient-centered healthcare systems. In: Proceedings of the 2020 4th International Conference on Cryptography, Security and Privacy, pp. 105–109 (2020)
5. GaushikM, R., JivteshM, R., Adarsh, P., Shibu, N., Rao, S.N.: A prototype design for gamified blood donation app using blockchain technology, IPFS and NFTS. In: Proceedings of the 20th ACM Conference on Embedded Networked Sensor Systems (2022)
6. Hawashin, D., Jayaraman, R., Salah, K., Yaqoob, I., Simsekler, M., Ellahham, S.: Blockchain-based management for organ donation and transplantation. IEEE Access **10**, 59013–59025 (2022)
7. Hawashin, D., Mahboobeh, D., Salah, K., Jayaraman, R., Yaqoob, I., Debe, M.S., Ellahham, S.: Blockchain-based management of blood donation. IEEE Access (2021)
8. Karthika, J., Keerthana, S., Shali, A.: Blockchain based transparent donating system (2023)
9. Le, H.T., et al.: Bloodchain: a blood donation network managed by blockchain technologies. Network **2**(1), 21–35 (2022)
10. Momaya, V.J.: Blockchain-based management for kidney donation and transplantation. J. Comput. Mech. Manag. (2023)
11. Momaya, V.J.: Revolutionizing organ donation with blockchain technology. J. Comput. Mech. Manag. **2**, 31–38 (2023)
12. Morande, S., Marzullo, M.: Application of artificial intelligence and blockchain in healthcare management-donor organ transplant system. Ann. Manag. Organ. Res. **1**(1), 25–38 (2019)
13. GN, Y.K. and Supreetha, M.: Smart NGO tracking system using blockchain technology. In: 2022 IEEE 2nd Mysore Sub Section International Conference (MysuruCon) (2022)
14. Ni, K., et al.: Barriers and facilitators to data quality of electronic health records used for clinical research in china: a qualitative study. BMJ Open **9**(7), e029314 (2019)
15. Parmar, K., Kumar, V.D., Prasanth, N.L., Pranoppal, Teja, K.C., Patil, S., Shah, K.A.: Blockchain based secure, efficient, and scalable platform for the organ donation process of healthcare industry. In: Hemanth, J., Pelusi, D., Chen, J.IZ. (eds.) International Conference on Intelligent Cyber Physical Systems and Internet of Things, vol. 3, pp. 173–183. Springer, Cham (2022). https://doi.org/10.1007/978-3-031-18497-0_13
16. Pawar, M.N.N., Wankhade, D.N.R.: Survey paper on : "organ donation using blockchain". Int. J. Adv. Res. Sci. Commun. Technol. 134–141 (2023)
17. Quynh, N.T.T., et al.: Toward a Design of Blood Donation Management by Blockchain Technologies. In: Gervasi, O., et al. (eds.) ICCSA 2021. LNCS, vol. 12956, pp. 78–90. Springer, Cham (2021). https://doi.org/10.1007/978-3-030-87010-2_6
18. Rai, S., Chaurasia, B., Gupta, R., Verma, S.: Blockchain-based NFT for healthcare system. In: 2023 IEEE 12th International Conference on Communication Systems and Network Technologies (CSNT) (2023)
19. Ranjan, P., Srivastava, S., Gupta, V., Tapaswi, S., Kumar, N.: Decentralised and distributed system for organ/tissue donation and transplantation. In: 2019 IEEE Conference on Information and Communication Technology (2019)

20. Soni, P., Mathur, A., Patel, D., R, M.: Blockchain-based organ donation platform: defeating trafficking and ensuring transparency. Int. Res. J. Adv. Sci. Hub **5**, 353–360 (2023)
21. Sumanth, B., Kavitha, M.K., MCA, M.: Management of organ donation and transplantation using blockchain. J. Eng. Sci. **14**(08) (2023)
22. Yahaya, C.A.C., Firdaus, A., Khen, Y.Y., Yaakub, C.Y., Abd Razak, M.F.: An organ donation management system (ODMS) based on blockchain technology for tracking and security purposes. In: 2021 International Conference on Software Engineering & Computer Systems and 4th International Conference on Computational Science and Information Management (ICSECS-ICOCSIM), pp. 377–382. IEEE (2021)

Proof of Stake Verifiers (PoSV) Consensus Mechanisms Implementation In AI Value Protocol (AIVP)

Adel ELMessiry[1(✉)] and Magdi El Messiry[2]

[1] WebDBTech, San Antonio, USA
Adel.ElMessiry@gmail.com
[2] Alexandria University, Alexandria, Egypt

Abstract. AIVP is designed to promote and incentivize value-driven AI projects through the use of blockchain technology. AI Value Protocol (AIVP) addresses this goal through a decentralized certification process driven by Proof of Stake Verifiers (PoSV) which is a blockchain-based consensus mechanism that relies on staked tokens to empower independent verifiers to assess AI projects for accuracy, performance, and ethical standards.

In this paper, we explore how PoSV within AIVP ensures fairness and transparency by requiring verifiers to stake tokens, tying their financial commitment to their performance. Verifiers independently evaluate AI projects and publish results, with consensus achieved through a majority vote, facilitated by the odd-number verifier system to prevent deadlock. This consensus-building process is central to AIVP's ability to certify AI systems without centralized oversight.

For verifiers, the system offers dual incentives: token rewards for accurate assessments and slashing penalties for dishonesty. In cases of disagreement, AIVP introduces an arbitration process, where verifiers can challenge outcomes by staking additional tokens, ensuring disputes are resolved fairly through re-evaluation by fresh verifiers.

Through these mechanisms, AIVP's PoSV system creates a robust, transparent framework for AI certification, ensuring only high-quality, ethically sound AI projects earn certification. We compare PoSV with other blockchain consensus models, demonstrating its unique suitability for decentralized AI verification. As AI continues to transform industries, AIVP offers a scalable, trust-driven solution to govern its development responsibly.

Keywords: AI · Artificial Intelligence · and Blockchain

1 Introduction

The swift expansion of artificial intelligence (AI) technologies has sparked a new wave of innovation and opportunities across numerous industries [3]. However,

S. He and L.-J. Zhang (Eds.): SCF/SCC 2024, LNCS 15430, pp. 47–59, 2025.
https://doi.org/10.1007/978-3-031-77000-5_4

this meteoric rise in AI adoption has brought to the forefront several critical challenges that the Artificial Intelligence Value Protocol (AIVP) aims to address [13] those issues.

2 AIVP Overview

AIVP is designed to promote and incentivize value-driven AI projects through the use of blockchain technology. The protocol aspires to become the leading platform for discovering, engaging with, and advancing verified AI initiatives that deliver genuine value. It will create a secure and verified environment where AI users and developers can seamlessly interact. The entire ecosystem is powered by the AIVP token, which functions as the backbone of this innovative platform. [5]:

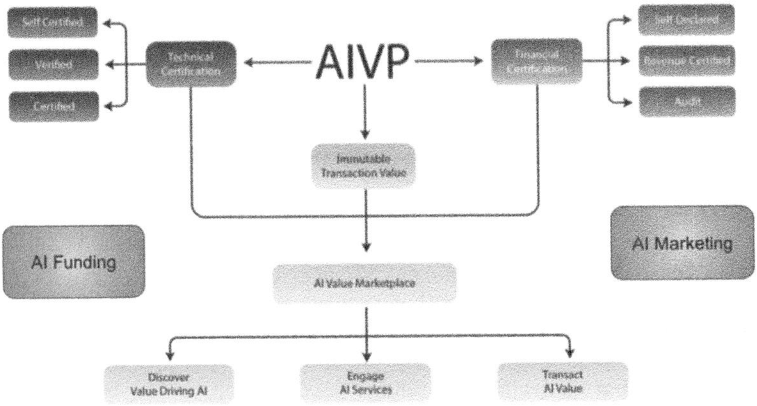

Fig. 1. AIVP Overview

2.1 Technical Certification

The technology certification process is centered on assessing the technical delivery of a project. It addresses the question: "Do the project's APIs produce the results they claim?" For example, if an AI project asserts that it can detect fraud in real-time, it must submit its algorithms for thorough verification before receiving certification. This transparency ensures that only legitimate AI projects receive AIVP certification, thereby maintaining trust within the ecosystem (Fig. 1).

Self-certification. Projects have the option to self-register and attest to their capabilities. Through self-certification, the project is assigned a unique blockchain address and identity. This entry-level certification is akin to how some ISO certifications permit companies to self-declare compliance with minimal oversight.

Verified Certification. Projects may request verification from the AIVP team to confirm the value they generate. This request is forwarded to available AIVP verifiers, requiring a minimum of three certified verifiers to reach a consensus on the verification. This level of certification is comparable to established models like SOC 2 Type 2 certifications, where auditors must assess and confirm a system's compliance with specific standards.

Certified. For AIVP certification, a project must provide full access to its algorithms, allowing AIVP verifiers to thoroughly examine and validate the technology. This level of transparency exceeds many traditional certification frameworks, ensuring a higher degree of accountability and trust.

2.2 AIVP Financial Certification

The financial certification process is focused on recording the actual value generated by a project. It consists of three levels: self-certified, revenue certified, and audited.

Financial Self-certification. Any project participating in the protocol can report its AI-generated value by calling the API or directly interacting with the smart contract using the generated value parameters and contributing 5% of the generated value. The smart contract records the value and returns 4.5% to the project in the form of AIVP tokens.

Revenue Certification. At the revenue certification level, projects submit the entire revenue from each delivered AI value to the protocol. The full value is tracked on the blockchain, and the protocol automatically deducts 5%, sending the remaining 95% to the project's designated wallet address. Additionally, 4.5% of the value is returned to the project wallet in the form of AIVP tokens, as is done with self-certification.

Full Audit Certification. In the full audit certification, an external accounting firm certifies the project's actual account payables. This firm reviews the project's payables and issues a Certificate before 95% of the revenue is returned to the project wallet. As with revenue certification, 4.5% of the value is automatically returned to the appropriate wallet in the form of AIVP tokens.

3 Consensus Algorithms

Blockchain networks rely on various consensus algorithms to ensure that all participants (nodes) agree on the state of the blockchain. These algorithms are crucial for maintaining the integrity, security, and decentralization of the network [4]. Let's review the most commonly used consensus algorithms:

1. Proof of Work (PoW)

- Overview: Proof of Work is the first and most well-known consensus algorithm, used by Bitcoin and other early cryptocurrencies. It requires nodes, known as miners, to solve complex mathematical puzzles to validate transactions and create new blocks [6].
- Process:
  - Miners compete to solve a cryptographic puzzle.
  - The first miner to solve the puzzle broadcasts the solution to the network.
  - Other nodes verify the solution, and if correct, the block is added to the blockchain.
  - The winning miner is rewarded with newly created cryptocurrency (block reward) and transaction fees.
- Strengths: High security and proven reliability.
- Weaknesses: Energy-intensive and can lead to centralization due to the need for specialized hardware.

2. Proof of Stake (PoS)

- Overview: Proof of Stake is an alternative to PoW that selects validators based on the number of tokens they hold and are willing to "stake" as collateral. It is used by networks like Ethereum 2.0 and Cardano [9].
- Process:
  - Validators are chosen to create new blocks based on the amount of cryptocurrency they stake.
  - The selected validator creates the next block and broadcasts it to the network.
  - Other validators verify the block, and if consensus is reached, the block is added to the blockchain.
  - Validators receive transaction fees as a reward, and in some cases, a portion of newly minted tokens.
- Strengths: Energy-efficient and reduces the need for specialized hardware.
- Weaknesses: Can lead to wealth centralization, where wealthy participants have more influence.

3. Delegated Proof of Stake (DPoS)

- Overview: Delegated Proof of Stake is a variation of PoS where stakeholders vote to elect a small number of delegates (or witnesses) who are responsible for validating transactions and maintaining the blockchain. It is used by networks like EOS and TRON [12].
- Process:
  - Token holders vote for a fixed number of delegates.
  - The elected delegates take turns producing and validating blocks.
  - If a delegate fails to perform their duties, they can be voted out and replaced.

  - Delegates are rewarded with transaction fees and, in some cases, new tokens.
- Strengths: Faster transaction processing and greater scalability.
- Weaknesses: Less decentralized, as a small group of delegates controls the network.

4. Proof of Authority (PoA)

- Overview: Proof of Authority is a consensus mechanism where a limited number of pre-approved nodes, known as authorities, validate transactions. It is commonly used in private or consortium blockchains like VeChain and some Ethereum-based networks [8].
- Process:
  - Only designated authorities are allowed to validate transactions and create new blocks.
  - These authorities are typically known and trusted entities.
  - The network relies on the reputation and trustworthiness of the authorities to maintain security.
- Strengths: High efficiency and low energy consumption.
- Weaknesses: Centralized, with trust placed in a few known entities.

5. Practical Byzantine Fault Tolerance (PBFT)

- Overview: PBFT is designed to function effectively in environments where nodes may fail or act maliciously. It is used by blockchains like Hyperledger Fabric and Zilliqa [7].
- Process:
  - A leader node is selected to propose the next block.
  - Other nodes, known as replicas, validate the proposal and broadcast their agreement or disagreement.
  - Once a sufficient number of nodes agree, the block is added to the blockchain.
  - The leader role rotates among nodes to prevent any single point of failure.
- Strengths: High fault tolerance and good performance in a controlled environment.
- Weaknesses: Limited scalability and higher communication overhead.

6. Proof of Burn (PoB)

- Overview: Proof of Burn requires participants to "burn" (destroy) a certain amount of cryptocurrency to earn the right to mine or validate transactions. It is seen as a more energy-efficient alternative to PoW [1].
- Process:
  - Miners burn tokens by sending them to an irretrievable address.
  - The act of burning tokens is recorded on the blockchain, and miners are granted the right to validate transactions.

  - The more tokens a miner burns, the greater their chance of being selected to create the next block.
- Strengths: Energy-efficient and reduces the reliance on physical resources.
- Weaknesses: Destruction of value and potentially limited long-term participation.

7. Proof of Space (PoSp) or Proof of Capacity (PoC)

- Overview: Proof of Space or Proof of Capacity involves using available hard drive space to validate transactions. It is used by networks like Chia [11].
- Process:
  - Miners allocate a portion of their hard drive space to the network.
  - The network uses this space to store cryptographic data, which is used to validate transactions.
  - The more space a miner allocates, the higher their chance of being selected to create the next block.
- Strengths: Lower energy consumption compared to PoW.
- Weaknesses: Still requires significant storage resources, which could lead to centralization.

8. Proof of Elapsed Time (PoET)

- Overview: Proof of Elapsed Time is a consensus mechanism that uses a trusted computing environment to ensure fairness in block creation. It is used by Hyperledger Sawtooth [2].
- Process:
  - Each node waits for a randomly assigned amount of time before proposing a new block.
  - The node with the shortest wait time creates the block and broadcasts it to the network.
  - The random wait time is generated by a trusted execution environment (TEE), ensuring fairness.
- Strengths: Energy-efficient and highly scalable.
- Weaknesses: Relies on trusted hardware, which may raise security concerns.

Different blockchain networks use various consensus algorithms based on their specific goals, trade-offs, and environments. Each algorithm has its strengths and weaknesses, which influence factors such as security, decentralization, energy efficiency, and scalability. Understanding these differences is crucial for choosing the appropriate blockchain platform for a given application or industry.

4 Proof of Stake Verifiers (PoSV) in AIVP

The Proof of Stake Verifiers (PoSV) system is a crucial component of the AI Value Protocol (AIVP), designed to ensure the integrity and reliability of the verification process while aligning the incentives of verifiers with the overall success of the network (Fig. 2).

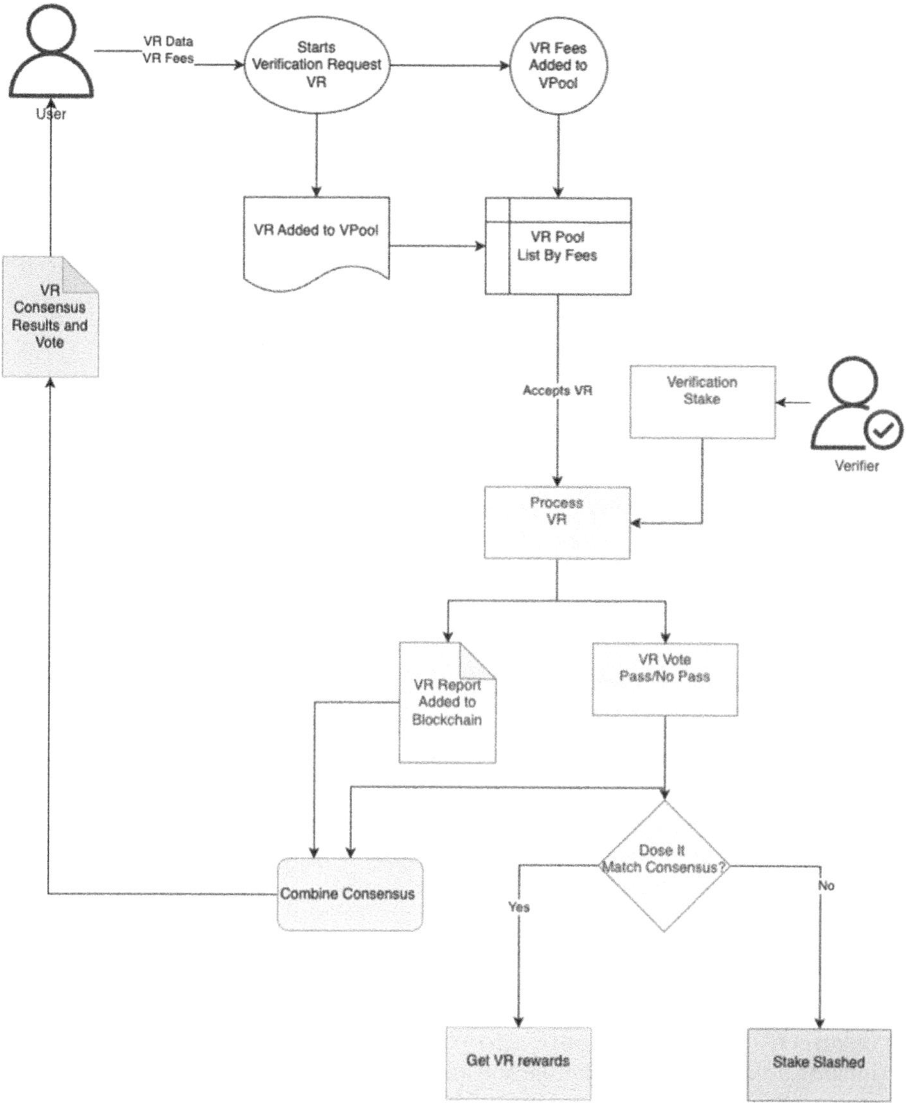

Fig. 2. PoSV Overview

4.1 Staking Requirement

Participation in Verification Pool: To become a verifier in the AIVP ecosystem, participants must stake a specific amount of AIVP tokens. This staking requirement acts as a security deposit, ensuring that only serious and committed verifiers participate in the process. The staked tokens serve as collateral, which can be slashed in the event of dishonest or incorrect behavior, thus aligning the verifier's incentives with the accuracy and honesty of their work.

4.2 Verification Request (VR) Process

- Odd Number of Verifiers: When a Verification Request (VR) is initiated, it is sent to the verification pool, where it is only accepted if an odd number of verifiers agree to take on the task. This odd number requirement helps prevent ties in voting, ensuring that a clear consensus can be reached.
- Publication of Results and Voting: Each verifier is required to independently assess the VR and publish their verification results alongside their vote. This transparency allows for the comparison of different verifiers' assessments and contributes to the overall trustworthiness of the process.

4.3 Consensus and Rewards

- Reaching Consensus: Once the verifiers have published their results and votes, the system checks for consensus. If a majority agrees, the consensus is recorded, and the VR is considered successfully verified [10].
- Distribution of Rewards: The rewards for successful verification are distributed among the verifiers who participated in the consensus. This reward is paid out in AIVP tokens, providing a financial incentive for accurate and honest verification.

4.4 Slashing Mechanism

Penalty for Failed Verifiers: Verifiers who fail to align with the consensus or are found to have provided incorrect verification results face penalties in the form of slashing their staked tokens. The slashing starts at 10% for the first failure and increases exponentially with subsequent failures. This slashing mechanism discourages dishonest behavior and ensures that only verifiers who are confident in their assessments participate.

4.5 Arbitration Process

- Requesting Arbitration: If a verifier believes that the consensus reached was incorrect, they have the option to request arbitration. To do so, they must initiate a vote and stake double the amount of their original stake. This higher stake reflects the increased risk and responsibility associated with challenging the initial consensus.
- New Set of Verifiers: The arbitration request (AR) triggers a new verification process with a different set of verifiers. These new verifiers re-evaluate the VR to determine if the initial consensus was indeed correct or if an error was made.
- Arbitration Outcomes: If the arbitration is successful, meaning the original consensus is overturned, the verifier who initiated the AR receives all the rewards from the verification process. In contrast, the verifiers who were part of the original, incorrect consensus will have their stakes slashed. If the AR fails, meaning the original consensus is upheld, the verifier who initiated the AR faces the maximum penalty, with their entire stake being slashed.

The PoSV mechanism within AIVP is carefully designed to ensure the integrity of the verification process, align verifier incentives with accuracy and honesty, and provide a clear pathway for resolving disputes. This system enhances the overall reliability and security of the AI Value Protocol, making it a robust platform for AI verification and certification.

5 Advantages of PoSV Consensus Mechanism

The Proof of Stake Verifiers (PoSV) mechanism is specifically designed for the unique needs of the AI Value Protocol (AIVP), making it more suitable than the general consensus algorithms used in traditional blockchain networks. Here's why PoSV is the optimal choice for AIVP:

1. Specialized for AI Verification. Tailored Verification Process: PoSV is specifically designed to handle the rigorous and nuanced requirements of AI verification, which involves complex assessments of AI models, data integrity, and ethical considerations. Unlike general consensus mechanisms like PoW or PoS, which focus on basic transaction validation, PoSV ensures that the verification process is carried out by knowledgeable and incentivized participants who understand the intricacies of AI.

2. Alignment of Incentives. Stake-Driven Accuracy: In PoSV, verifiers must stake AIVP tokens to participate in the verification process. This staking mechanism ensures that verifiers have a financial interest in providing accurate and honest verification. If they fail to align with the consensus or act dishonestly, their stake is slashed, starting at 10% and increasing with repeated failures. This strong financial incentive ensures that only serious and reliable participants engage in the verification process, enhancing the overall integrity of AIVP.

3. Flexibility in Arbitration. Dispute Resolution: PoSV includes a built-in arbitration mechanism that allows verifiers to challenge a consensus if they believe it is incorrect. This is not typically available in other consensus mechanisms like PoW, PoS, or DPoS, where the finality of blocks is more rigid. In PoSV, a verifier can initiate arbitration by staking double the amount, triggering a re-evaluation by a new set of verifiers. This flexibility ensures that the system can self-correct and maintain high standards of accuracy and fairness, which is crucial for AI certification and verification.

4. Decentralization with Accountability. Distributed Verification with Individual Accountability: While other consensus mechanisms aim to decentralize decision-making, PoSV adds an extra layer of accountability by requiring verifiers to publicly publish their verification results alongside their votes. This transparency ensures that all actions are traceable and that verifiers can be held accountable for their decisions. In contrast, mechanisms like DPoS concentrate power among a few elected delegates, which can reduce overall accountability and increase the risk of collusion.

5. Optimized for AI Projects. Focus on AI's Unique Requirements: The general consensus mechanisms mentioned above are designed for broader applications, such as cryptocurrency transactions or general-purpose blockchains. PoSV, however, is optimized specifically for the AI ecosystem. It is built to handle the unique challenges posed by AI projects, such as the need for continuous validation, ethical considerations, and the assessment of AI's real-world impact.

6. Enhanced Security and Fraud Mitigation. Slashing and Reward Mechanisms: PoSV's slashing mechanism for failed verifications and the potential for arbitration make it highly secure and resistant to fraud. This is particularly important in the context of AI, where the consequences of incorrect verification can be significant. Other consensus mechanisms, like PoW or PoS, do not offer such targeted fraud mitigation tailored to the verification of complex AI systems.

7. Scalability and Efficiency. Efficient Consensus for AI Verification: Unlike PoW, which is resource-intensive and slow, or DPoS, which may suffer from centralization issues, PoSV is designed to be both efficient and scalable. It allows AIVP to process a large number of AI verification requests without compromising on security or decentralization. This balance is crucial for a protocol that aims to scale across various industries and use cases.

6 Conclusion

The AI Value Protocol (AIVP) represents a groundbreaking approach to ensuring the integrity, reliability, and incentivization of AI verification and certification processes. By leveraging the decentralized power of blockchain technology, AIVP offers a transparent, secure, and robust framework that aligns the interests of all participants-users, verifiers, and stakeholders alike.

Key features such as the Proof of Stake Verifiers (PoSV) system, Horus Wallet integration for seamless user authentication, and the use of advanced consensus mechanisms on fast blockchains like Base and Polygon, all contribute to AIVP's resilience and effectiveness. The protocol's commitment to privacy, security, and fault tolerance further underscores its capacity to operate reliably under a wide range of conditions.

AIVP's innovative governance and arbitration processes ensure that the network remains fair and just, providing clear pathways for dispute resolution and maintaining the finality and immutability of records. These measures, combined with a strong focus on interoperability, performance, and resource sustainability, position AIVP as a leading solution in the emerging field of AI value verification.

PoSV is not just another consensus algorithm; it is a mechanism specifically crafted to meet the demands of AI verification and certification within the AIVP. It combines the strengths of staking-based incentives, rigorous verification processes, flexibility in dispute resolution, and accountability to create a system that is uniquely suited to the challenges of the AI landscape. Using PoSV in AIVP ensures that the protocol can deliver high-quality, trustworthy AI assessments, which are critical for fostering trust and transparency in AI technologies.

In conclusion, AIVP not only addresses the current challenges in AI verification but also sets a new standard for how AI systems can be evaluated, certified, and incentivized in a decentralized and trustless environment. Through its carefully designed protocols and strategic use of blockchain technology, AIVP is poised to become a cornerstone in the future of AI governance, offering unparalleled reliability and security in the certification of AI systems.

Acknowledgment. The authors would like to acknowledge AlphaFin, WebDBTech, Health Reasoning, Ahmed Akram, and Open AI for their support.

A Key Terminology

In order to facilitate a clearer understanding of the concepts discussed in this paper, the following definitions provide explanations of the blockchain-specific terms used within the AI Value Protocol (AIVP).

A.1 Blockchain

A decentralized, distributed ledger that records transactions across multiple computers. Blockchain technology ensures that records are secure, immutable, and verifiable without relying on a centralized authority. In the context of AIVP, blockchain is used to securely record the verification and certification of AI projects.

A.2 Immutability

Once data is recorded on the blockchain, it cannot be altered or deleted. This feature ensures that records, such as AI project certifications, remain permanent and tamper-proof. Immutability enhances trust, as stakeholders know the data has not been changed.

A.3 Decentralization

The process of distributing data and control across a network rather than relying on a single central authority. In AIVP, decentralization means that no single entity has control over the verification or certification process, reducing the risk of bias or manipulation.

A.4 Smart Contracts

Self-executing contracts with the terms of the agreement written directly into code. In AIVP, smart contracts automate certification processes and token rewards, ensuring that actions occur automatically when predefined conditions are met. This removes the need for intermediaries and reduces errors.

A.5 Proof of Stake (PoS)

A consensus mechanism used in blockchain where validators (or verifiers) are selected to confirm transactions or data based on the number of tokens they hold and are willing to "stake." In AIVP, PoS ensures that only serious participants with a financial commitment are involved in the verification of AI projects.

A.6 Slashing

A penalty mechanism used in Proof of Stake systems where a portion of the staked tokens is forfeited by a verifier if they act dishonestly or fail to perform their duties accurately. In AIVP, slashing discourages verifiers from making inaccurate or biased assessments during the AI project certification process.

A.7 Consensus

The agreement among participants in a decentralized network about the validity of data or transactions. In the AIVP, a consensus is required among verifiers to certify an AI project. Consensus is necessary to ensure that the verification process is unbiased and trustworthy.

A.8 Arbitration

A process in which disputes over verification results are resolved. In AIVP, verifiers can request arbitration if they believe the consensus reached is incorrect. A new set of verifiers re-evaluates the data to determine the final outcome. This mechanism ensures fairness and accuracy in the certification process.

A.9 Staking

The act of locking up tokens as collateral to participate in blockchain activities, such as verification. In the AIVP, verifiers must stake AIVP tokens to take part in the certification process. If they behave dishonestly or fail, their staked tokens may be partially or fully forfeited (slashed).

A.10 Token Economics

The economic model governing the creation, distribution, and use of tokens within a blockchain ecosystem. In AIVP, tokens are used as a medium of exchange, for governance, and as rewards for participants who contribute to the verification and certification processes.

References

1. Aggarwal, S., Kumar, N.: Cryptographic consensus mechanisms. In: Advances in Computers, vol. 121, pp. 211–226. Elsevier (2021)
2. Chen, L., Xu, L., Shah, N., Gao, Z., Lu, Y., Shi, W.: On security analysis of proof-of-elapsed-time (PoET). In: Spirakis, P., Tsigas, P. (eds.) SSS 2017. LNCS, vol. 10616, pp. 282–297. Springer, Cham (2017). https://doi.org/10.1007/978-3-319-69084-1_19
3. ElMessiry, A., ElMessiry, M., Spiceland, D.: Leveraging the artificial intelligence value protocol (AIVP) for educational enhancement. In: EDULEARN24 Proceedings, pp. 7099–7103. 16th International Conference on Education and New Learning Technologies, IATED, 1-3 July 2024 (2024). https://doi.org/10.21125/edulearn.2024.1679
4. ElMessiry, M., ElMessiry, A.: Blockchain framework for textile supply chain management. In: Chen, S., Wang, H., Zhang, L.-J. (eds.) ICBC 2018. LNCS, vol. 10974, pp. 213–227. Springer, Cham (2018). https://doi.org/10.1007/978-3-319-94478-4_15
5. ElMessiry, M., ElMessiry, A., ElMessiry, M.: Dual token blockchain economy framework. In: Joshi, J., Nepal, S., Zhang, Q., Zhang, L.-J. (eds.) ICBC 2019. LNCS, vol. 11521, pp. 157–170. Springer, Cham (2019). https://doi.org/10.1007/978-3-030-23404-1_11
6. Gemeliarana, I.G.A.K., Sari, R.F.: Evaluation of proof of work (pow) blockchains security network on selfish mining. In: 2018 International seminar on research of information technology and intelligent systems (ISRITI), pp. 126–130. IEEE (2018)
7. Li, Y., Qiao, L., Lv, Z.: An optimized byzantine fault tolerance algorithm for consortium blockchain. Peer-to-Peer Netw. Appl. **14**, 2826–2839 (2021)
8. Manolache, M.A., Manolache, S., Tapus, N.: Decision making using the blockchain proof of authority consensus. Procedia Comput. Sci. **199**, 580–588 (2022)
9. Saleh, F.: Blockchain without waste: proof-of-stake. Rev. Finan. Stud. **34**(3), 1156–1190 (2021)
10. Shifferaw, Y., Lemma, S.: Limitations of proof of stake algorithm in blockchain: a review. Zede J. **39**(1), 81–95 (2021)
11. Verma, N., Jain, S., Doriya, R.: Review on consensus protocols for blockchain. In: 2021 International Conference on Computing, Communication, and Intelligent Systems (ICCCIS), pp. 281–286. IEEE (2021)
12. Yang, F., Zhou, W., Wu, Q., Long, R., Xiong, N.N., Zhou, M.: Delegated proof of stake with downgrade: a secure and efficient blockchain consensus algorithm with downgrade mechanism. IEEE access **7**, 118541–118555 (2019)
13. Zhao, Y., Yin, D., Wang, L., Yu, Y.: The rise of artificial intelligence, the fall of human wellbeing? Int. J. Soc. Welf. **33**(1), 75–105 (2024)

Blockchain-Based Insurance Claim Management: Implementing RSA-Encrypted NFTs for Sccurc and Transparent Processing

Trung Phan Huynh Tuan, K. Bang Le, Nghiem Pham Thanh, Bao Tran Quoc, Bang Ngo Hai, Anh T. Nguyen, Khiem Huynh Gia(✉), and Hung Nhat Nguyen

FPT University, Can Tho city, Vietnam
trungpht@fe.edu.vn, khiemhgce160922@fpt.edu.vn

Abstract. This paper investigates the application of blockchain technology in insurance claim management, focusing on the use of RSA-encrypted non-fungible tokens (NFTs) and smart contracts to address issues of transparency, security, and efficiency. Traditional insurance claim processes often involve complex and manual steps prone to errors, delays, and fraud. By implementing blockchain technology, we propose a system that automates these processes and ensures that all transactions are transparent and immutable. The study evaluates the performance of blockchain in automating claim processing, securing data, and reducing fraud. It also examines the economic aspects of using blockchain by analyzing transaction fees across several Ethereum Virtual Machine (EVM)-compatible platforms. The goal is to highlight the potential of blockchain to transform insurance claim management into a more efficient, secure, and transparent system.

Keywords: Blockchain · Transparency in insurance · Data Privacy and Security · Smart Contracts · Decentralized Marketplaces · RSA-Encrypted NFTs

1 Introduction

The integration of blockchain technology in various sectors has garnered significant attention due to its potential to enhance transparency, security, and efficiency. One such sector is insurance claim management, where blockchain can address long-standing issues related to fraud, inefficiencies, and lack of transparency. This paper explores the use of blockchain technology, specifically focusing on the implementation of RSA-encrypted non-fungible tokens (NFTs) and smart contracts, to improve the management of insurance claims.

Insurance claim management traditionally involves multiple steps, including claim submission, verification, processing, and settlement. These steps often require coordination among various entities, such as policyholders, insurance

S. He and L.-J. Zhang (Eds.): SCF/SCC 2024, LNCS 15430, pp. 60–73, 2025.
https://doi.org/10.1007/978-3-031-77000-5_5

companies, adjusters, and third-party service providers. The complexity and manual nature of these processes can lead to delays, errors, and opportunities for fraudulent activities. Blockchain technology offers a decentralized and tamper-proof platform that can streamline these processes, ensuring that all transactions are transparent and verifiable [5].

Previous studies have demonstrated the feasibility of blockchain-based solutions in various insurance applications. For instance, the "ClaimChain" system uses machine learning to automate claim processing and secure the platform against fraud and data integrity attacks, achieving high accuracy in fraud detection [4]. Similarly, "VehicleInsurance" leverages smart contracts to automate policy management and claims processing, significantly improving efficiency and customer experience by eliminating intermediaries [16]. These examples highlight the potential benefits of integrating blockchain technology into insurance claim management systems.

The use of RSA-encrypted NFTs in insurance claim management adds an additional layer of security and verifiability. NFTs serve as unique digital identifiers for insurance claims, encapsulating all relevant information in a tamper-proof format. By storing these NFTs on decentralized storage systems like the InterPlanetary File System (IPFS), the claim data remains secure and accessible to authorized parties. The use of smart contracts ensures that all claim-related transactions are automatically recorded on the blockchain, providing a transparent and immutable record of the entire process [2].

The economic efficiency of blockchain-based insurance claim management systems is another critical factor to consider. Transaction fees associated with blockchain operations, such as data creation, NFT minting, and NFT transfer, significantly impact the overall cost-effectiveness of these systems. A comparative analysis of transaction fees across various Ethereum Virtual Machine (EVM)-compatible platforms, including BNB Chain, Fantom, Polygon, and Celo, reveals differences in fee structures and highlights the importance of selecting a cost-effective platform for implementation [6].

This paper aims to provide a comprehensive evaluation of the implementation of RSA-encrypted NFTs and smart contracts in insurance claim management. We conduct a detailed performance analysis, focusing on the encryption and decryption of claim-related data and the associated computational costs. Additionally, we assess the economic efficiency of different blockchain platforms by analyzing transaction fees for key operations. Our goal is to identify a blockchain solution that balances security, transparency, and cost-effectiveness, thereby enhancing the overall efficiency of insurance claim management systems.

In the subsequent sections, we will discuss the methodology used for our analysis, present the results of our performance evaluation, and provide insights into the practical implications of our findings. By doing so, we aim to contribute to the ongoing research on blockchain applications in insurance and provide a framework for future implementations that can further improve the transparency and efficiency of insurance claim management.

2 Related Work

2.1 Integration of Blockchain in Insurance Claims Management

Blockchain technology has been increasingly adopted to improve transparency and streamline processes in insurance claim management. A study illustrated a blockchain-based method for managing and analyzing data within a pay-as-you-go auto insurance model, ensuring all parties have clear and traceable data access [17]. Another research introduced EthInsurance, a system designed to uphold transparency between health insurers and policyholders by removing intermediaries and providing secure medical data access [14]. The CioSy system utilizes blockchain to facilitate the automation of insurance policy processing and claim management via smart contracts, offering a secure environment resistant to tampering [12]. Further, research integrating machine learning with blockchain has shown effectiveness in verifying insurance claims and identifying fraudulent activities, with significant accuracy in detecting fraud [2]. An additional review of blockchain applications within the insurance sector has underlined the benefits of using smart contracts for claims processing, underwriting, and fraud prevention, while also noting the challenges related to scalability and compliance [5]. Collectively, these findings underscore blockchain's role in fostering more transparent, streamlined, and secure environments for insurance operations.

The adoption of blockchain technology in managing insurance claims has proven effective in boosting both transparency and operational efficiency. For instance, the "ClaimChain" system leverages machine learning to automate claim processing and bolster security against fraud and data integrity issues, showing notable success in detecting fraudulent activities [4]. Similarly, the "VehicleInsurance" platform utilizes smart contracts for streamlining policy management and claim handling in vehicle insurance, significantly enhancing user experience and efficiency by removing the need for middlemen [16]. Moreover, various blockchain frameworks suggest the use of smart contracts for automating claims processing and decision-making processes, which could lead to cost reductions and compliance benefits [1]. The B-SAHIC system applies Hyperledger Fabric and smart contracts in health insurance claim management to ensure privacy and scalability, resulting in rapid and effective system performance [10]. Additionally, a structured approach for managing insurance transactions via blockchain-enabled smart contracts has been developed, aiming to improve transparency and efficiency across the insurance sector [6]. These examples collectively demonstrate how blockchain technology can revolutionize insurance claim management by making systems more transparent, efficient, and secure.

2.2 Healthcare and Privacy Protection

The referenced research collectively explores blockchain technology's role in enhancing the privacy and security of healthcare systems. These studies delve into various applications related to healthcare, such as managing patient data, ensuring the secure exchange of personal health information, and incorporating artificial intelligence, highlighting the effectiveness of blockchain in handling sensitive health information.

Bang et al. [3] present a Hyperledger Fabric-based Internet of Healthcare Things (IoHT) platform that allows secure and transparent patient data management. This platform uses smart contracts to enable patients to manage access to their data and connected devices, adhering to privacy conditions set by the patients themselves. The evaluation of this system demonstrates its capability to serve as a dependable solution for maintaining healthcare data privacy and management.

Duong et al. [7,8] concentrate on the incorporation of blockchain into patient-centric healthcare systems. They highlight the role of smart contracts in enhancing data privacy, trust between providers, and system interoperability. Their work details the architecture and functionality of components within healthcare systems that allow patients to securely manage and share their health records. Their findings offer practical insights and algorithms for secure healthcare information management, illustrating effective strategies for patient data handling.

Le et al. [11] and Quynh et al. [13] have developed blockchain-based frameworks for blood donation systems. These frameworks utilize private blockchain technology to manage critical data regarding the quality, availability, and demand for blood, aiming to enhance the efficiency and clarity of managing blood resources, thus improving overall healthcare logistics and supply chain processes.

Shinde et al. [15] investigate how blockchain technology can be integrated with AI-driven healthcare systems. Their review highlights blockchain's potential to boost security and reliability within AI applications in healthcare. They outline a theoretical framework employing blockchain to safeguard against adversarial attacks and maintain data privacy and traceability, tackling key concerns around security and transparency in AI-driven decision-making.

Zheng et al. [18] and Grishin et al. [9] explore the utilization of blockchain for personal health and genomic data sharing. Zheng et al. discuss a model that merges blockchain with cloud storage to facilitate health data sharing, prioritizing user control and compliance with GDPR guidelines. Conversely, Grishin et al. propose a decentralized strategy for genomic data sharing that incorporates privacy-preserving technologies and blockchain to enhance data accessibility and ensure fair compensation, addressing economic and privacy issues associated with genomic sequencing.

3 Approach

3.1 Phase One: Enhancing Transparency in an Insurance Claim Management System: A Blockchain-Enabled Platform and RSA-Encrypted NFTs

The image Fig. 1 outlines a detailed workflow of an insurance claim management system that leverages blockchain technology for better handling and tracking of

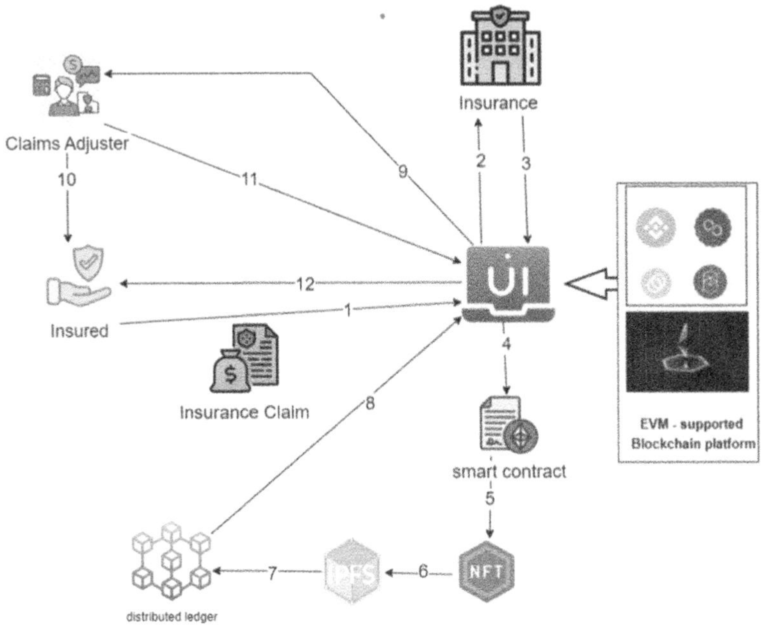

Fig. 1. Workflow of blockchain-based personal data marketplace

claims. The process involves multiple steps and interactions among different entities to ensure that claims are processed efficiently and transparently.

The process initiates when the insured individual submits an insurance claim through a user interface (UI). This interface acts as the central point for claim submission, allowing the insured to input all necessary details and documents related to their claim. Once the claim is submitted, the UI forwards the claim to the insurance company for further verification. This step is crucial as it involves the insurance company's internal processes to validate the claim's authenticity and ensure all required information is provided.

Upon receiving the claim from the UI, the insurance company undertakes a thorough verification process. This involves checking the claim details against the policy terms and conditions, evaluating the provided documentation, and possibly conducting additional investigations if necessary. After completing this verification, the insurance company communicates the verification results back to the UI. This step ensures that the UI has the latest status of the claim, which can then be used for further processing.

The UI, equipped to handle interactions with blockchain technology, processes the information received from the insurance company. It interacts with a smart contract deployed on an Ethereum Virtual Machine (EVM)-supported blockchain platform. The smart contract contains predefined logic that governs the handling of the claim. It executes this logic, which could involve steps such as calculating claim amounts, verifying conditions, and updating claim statuses.

As a result of this execution, the smart contract generates a non-fungible token (NFT) that represents the claim. This NFT serves as a unique digital identifier for the claim, encapsulating all relevant information in a tamper-proof format.

Once the NFT is generated, it is stored on the InterPlanetary File System (IPFS). IPFS is a decentralized storage system that allows data to be stored across a network of nodes, ensuring that the information is both secure and accessible. Storing the NFT on IPFS ensures that the claim data is not reliant on a single point of failure and can be retrieved by any authorized party. The IPFS hash, which uniquely identifies the stored data, is then recorded in a distributed ledger. This ledger acts as a transparent and immutable record of all transactions and data related to the claim, ensuring that all parties have access to a consistent and tamper-proof record.

After the claim data is stored and the IPFS hash is recorded in the distributed ledger, the UI retrieves updated information from the smart contract. This updated information includes the latest status of the claim and any actions that need to be taken. The UI updates the insurance claim status accordingly and provides this information back to the insurance company. This step ensures that the insurance company is always aware of the current status of the claim and can take any necessary actions based on this information.

The insurance company, upon receiving the updated claim status from the UI, communicates with the claims adjuster. The claims adjuster is responsible for reviewing the claim details, which may involve examining the claim documentation, conducting interviews, and assessing the claim's validity. The claims adjuster might also need to interact directly with the insured to gather additional information or clarify any ambiguities. Once the review is complete, the claims adjuster updates the claim status on the UI, providing any necessary notes or instructions for further processing.

Finally, the insured is notified of the claim status and any required follow-up actions. This notification includes detailed information about the claim's current status, any decisions made by the insurance company, and any additional steps the insured needs to take. This comprehensive and transparent process ensures that the insured is always kept informed about their claim and can respond promptly to any requests or updates. By integrating blockchain technology, this system aims to improve the efficiency and transparency of the insurance claim process, ensuring that all steps are recorded and accessible to all involved parties.

3.2 Phase Two: Integration of RSA-Encrypted NFTs and Smart Contracts for Enhancing Transparency in an Insurance Claim Management System

The image Fig. 2 illustrates the workflow of an insurance claim management system using blockchain technology and RSA-encrypted NFTs. This system involves several steps and interactions among different entities to ensure that claims are processed accurately and transparently.

The process begins with the insured individual submitting an insurance claim. This claim submission generates a document containing all relevant details

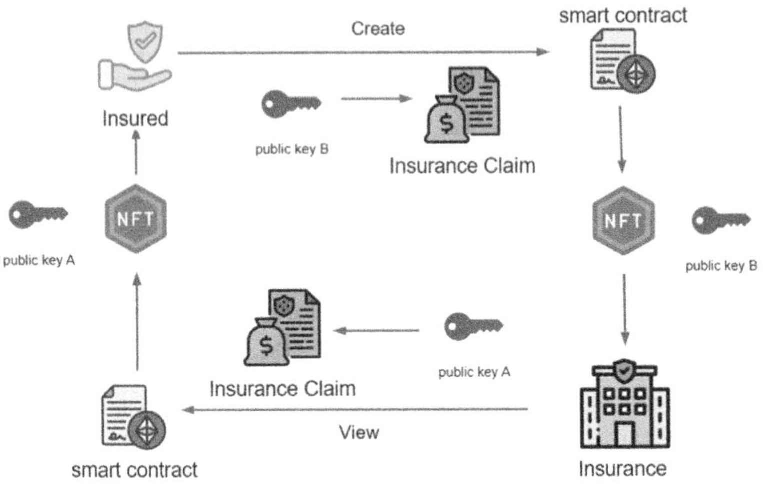

Fig. 2. Workflow of blockchain-based personal data marketplace

and necessary information. The document is then forwarded to a smart contract on a blockchain platform, which supports Ethereum Virtual Machine (EVM). The smart contract verifies and processes the claim information.

As part of this processing, the smart contract creates a non-fungible token (NFT) representing the insurance claim. This NFT is unique and serves as a digital identifier for the claim. The public key B, associated with the insurance company, is used during this process to ensure secure handling of the claim information.

Once the NFT is generated, it is stored and linked to the public key B, allowing the insurance company to access and view the claim. The insurance company can review the claim details and, using the public key A, update the claim status or provide additional information as needed. This update is communicated back to the smart contract, which ensures that the information is recorded on the blockchain in a tamper-proof manner.

The insured can also view the claim status by interacting with the smart contract. They use public key A to securely access the claim information, ensuring that only authorized parties can view and manage the claim details. This process ensures that both the insurance company and the insured have access to the latest and most accurate claim status.

4 Evaluation

4.1 Assessing the Impact of RSA-Encrypted NFTs on Person Data Trading

A detailed performance evaluation was conducted to assess the application of RSA-Encrypted NFTs within an insurance claim management system. This study focused on two types of data essential for documenting claims: image files, used to verify the authenticity of data sources such as claim documents and accident photos, and text records, akin to transaction details and policy certifications commonly encountered in insurance processes. The objective of this evaluation was to determine the effectiveness of these digitally secured assets in managing and securing claim data, with an emphasis on enhancing transparency and security from the initial filing to the final processing of claims. This analysis sought to measure the impact of a blockchain-enabled platform equipped with RSA-Encrypted NFTs on improving transparency in the management of insurance claims, ensuring that data handling is secure and clear throughout the entire process.

The data in Table 1 offers a detailed assessment of the time efficiency, measured in microseconds, for RSA key generation, encryption, and decryption of image data within an insurance claim management system. The RSA key generation times vary significantly, with the fastest at 24,634 ms and the slowest at 82,146 ms, indicating a possible dependency on system resources or load at the time of key generation. Image encryption times are relatively lower, ranging from 5,391 to 13,854 ms, suggesting a more consistent and faster process. However, the decryption times are considerably higher, all exceeding 178,515 ms, with a peak at 197,697 ms, highlighting the computational intensity of the RSA decryption process. This table underscores the trade-off between robust security, provided by RSA encryption, and the considerable time required for decryption, which could impact system performance and user experience in real-time scenarios.

Table 1. Evaluation of Time Efficiency in RSA Key Generation, Encryption, and Decryption for Image in Microseconds

RSA (image)	1	2	3	4	5	6	7	8	9	10
Generating key	38572	38298	42582	82146	54130	51060	45893	28499	24634	68740
Encrypting image	6291	13854	6734	11037	10501	5391	8660	11455	10596	9769
Decrypting image	183250	186500	183974	179189	190492	178515	186146	197697	185491	195150

Table 2 presents the time efficiency metrics for RSA key generation, encryption, and decryption of text data in microseconds, showcasing considerable variation across different trials within an insurance claim management system. Key generation times are notably inconsistent, ranging from 31,123 to 99,402 ms, reflecting potential variations in computational load or algorithmic efficiency during each trial. Interestingly, the encryption times for text show an anomaly where most trials recorded zero microseconds, except for the first trial at 112 ms, suggesting possible measurement errors or exceptionally efficient encryption processes under specific conditions. Decryption times, while mostly recorded as zero, show sporadic nonzero values (800 to 1,043 ms), indicating occasional delays in processing. This table highlights the erratic nature of encryption and decryption times for text, potentially affecting the system's overall performance in processing claims data securely and efficiently.

Table 2. Evaluation of Time Efficiency in RSA Key Generation, Encryption, and Decryption for Text in Microseconds

RSA (text)	1	2	3	4	5	6	7	8	9	10
Generating key	85730	52907	45749	31123	66118	94909	62376	99402	68911	79471
Encrypting text	112	0	0	0	0	0	0	0	0	0
Decrypting text	800	0	0	0	1043	0	1001	1007	1024	0

Performance metrics indicate that RSA encryption maintains consistent effectiveness across various data types, with key generation and decryption phases proving particularly resource-intensive. This reflects the algorithm's emphasis on strong security measures. The extended time required for decryption highlights the considerable computational effort necessary to access secured data in RSA-encrypted frameworks. Within an insurance claim management system, finding the right balance between robust security and processing efficiency is crucial. Effective management of this balance ensures that claim data is both protected and processed efficiently. The implementation of RSA encryption in such a system needs to carefully weigh data security against operational speed to maintain both the integrity and transparency of insurance claim transactions on a blockchain-enabled platform.

4.2 Testing on the Four EVM-Supported Platforms

The management of insurance claim data using blockchain technology requires careful consideration of transaction fees, as these fees significantly influence the operational costs and scalability of blockchain solutions. This section presents a comparative analysis of transaction fees across four Ethereum Virtual Machine (EVM)-compatible platforms: BNB Chain, Fantom, Polygon, and Celo. We assess each platform's fee structure to determine its suitability for implementing cost-effective, blockchain-based systems for insurance claim management, focusing on cost-effectiveness and functionality in various operational contexts.

This study explores how blockchain technology can enhance the management of insurance claim systems, integrating RSA-encrypted NFTs and IPFS into the system. The analysis highlights three critical functions: data creation, NFT minting, and NFT transfer. These functions are crucial for recording claims, verifying the authenticity of documents, and securely distributing digital assets among participants.

In evaluating the practicality and performance of these platforms, we focus on the aforementioned four EVM-compatible blockchain platforms: BNB Chain, Fantom, Celo, and Polygon. Each platform is examined for its ability to support key operations necessary for efficient management of insurance claims. Special attention is given to the efficiency and cost-effectiveness of the transaction processes, aiding in the selection of the most suitable platforms for establishing robust and transparent systems in insurance claim management.

4.3 Results

The analysis of transaction fees is crucial for evaluating blockchain-based systems, especially within the context of insurance claim management. These fees significantly affect the economic viability and sustainability of the system for all users, compensating validators or miners for securing the network and processing transactions.

Our evaluation focuses on three essential operations integral to the functionality of platforms managing insurance claims using RSA-encrypted NFTs: data/transaction creation, minting RSA-encrypted NFTs, and transferring RSA-encrypted NFTs. Each of these functions plays a key role in the lifecycle of an insurance claim on the blockchain:

1. Data or transaction creation involves recording information about insurance claims on the blockchain. This step ensures that details regarding claim transactions are permanently and transparently stored, which directly influences the cost for users to tokenize their claim data.
2. Minting of RSA-encrypted NFTs transforms insurance claim details into unique digital assets—RSA-encrypted NFTs-that signify ownership or certification of the claim. This process is essential for the digital representation of claims, enabling them to be managed more efficiently. Analyzing the fees for minting RSA-encrypted NFTs is crucial to keep the process affordable and accessible for users, thus supporting the operational efficiency of the insurance claim management system.
3. The transfer of RSA-encrypted NFTs involves the exchange of ownership of these digital assets between parties. This function is central to the management platform, facilitating the movement and distribution of claim data. The costs associated with RSA-encrypted NFT transfers affect the liquidity and ease of transactions within the system. High transfer fees might limit the frequency of transactions and reduce system utilization, while lower fees could encourage more active management and resolution of claims.

By examining the fees associated with these three functions, we gain insights into the overall efficiency and cost-effectiveness of the blockchain platform for insurance claim management. This examination allows us to compare different blockchain networks and select the most suitable platform based on the balance between operational costs and network performance. The goal is to find a blockchain solution that provides necessary functionality at the lowest possible cost, maximizing benefits for all participants in the insurance claim management ecosystem.

Table 3. Transaction fee

	Transaction Creation	Create NFT	Transfer NFT
BNB	0.0273134 BNB ($16.47)	0.00109162 BNB ($0.66)	0.00057003 BNB ($0.34)
Fantom	0.00957754 FTM ($0.00)	0.000405167 FTM ($0.00)	0.0002380105 FTM ($0.00)
Polygon	0.006840710032835408 MATIC ($0.01)	0.000289405001852192 MATIC ($0.00)	0.000170007501088048 MATIC ($0.00)
Celo	0.007097844 CELO ($0.005)	0.0002840812 CELO ($0.000)	0.0001554878 CELO ($0.000)

Transaction Fee Analysis. Table 3 provides a comparative analysis of transaction fees for three key operations on four Ethereum Virtual Machine (EVM)-compatible blockchain platforms: BNB Chain, Fantom, Polygon, and Celo, with token prices recorded on May 27, 2024. These operations include creating transactions, minting RSA-encrypted NFTs, and transferring RSA-encrypted NFTs, all essential for the management and security of insurance claim data using blockchain technology. By evaluating the fee structures of each platform, we can assess their economic efficiency and suitability for use in systems designed for the transparent management of insurance claims through blockchain, RSA-encrypted NFTs, smart contracts, and IPFS.

BNB Chain imposes a relatively high fee for transaction creation at 0.0273134 BNB, approximately $16.47, which might deter frequent transaction activities in systems with high operational volume. Despite this, the fees associated with NFT creation and transfer are substantially lower at 0.00109162 BNB ($0.66) and 0.00057003 BNB ($0.34) respectively. This differential pricing indicates that while initiating transactions on BNB Chain might be costly, the subsequent steps involving NFT handling—crucial for representing insurance claim data-are much more economically feasible. Therefore, BNB Chain could be well-suited for scenarios where initial claim entries are infrequent, but subsequent claim handling and updates involving NFTs are more common.

Fantom presents a highly competitive fee structure, especially attractive for systems that demand high-frequency operations. It charges a nominal fee of only 0.00957754 FTM for transaction creation. For NFT creation and transfer, the fees drop to 0.000405167 FTM and 0.0002380105 FTM respectively, which are almost negligible. This fee structure makes Fantom an ideal platform for insurance claim management systems that require continuous updates to claims and frequent transfers of claim data, as the cost implications are minimal, promoting more dynamic and responsive claim processing.

Polygon is another platform that offers very low transaction fees, with a transaction creation fee of just 0.006840710032835408 MATIC, approximately $0.01. The fees for NFT creation and transfer are even lower, at 0.000289405001852192 MATIC and 0.000170007501088048 MATIC respectively, facilitating cost-effective scalability and frequent transaction processing. This fee structure benefits insurance claim management systems that handle a wide range of claims and associated data, allowing for economical scaling without compromising on the frequency of data transactions and updates.

Celo, targeting mobile accessibility and cost efficiency, charges 0.007097844 CELO (about $0.005) for transaction creation, with further reduced fees for NFT creation and transfer at 0.0002840812 CELO and 0.0001554878 CELO, respectively. This exceptionally low-cost structure is particularly advantageous for stakeholders in economically constrained regions, providing a viable solution for managing insurance claims efficiently and affordably. Celo's focus on low-cost transactions and mobile-first approach can significantly enhance accessibility and usability in global markets where cost and mobile accessibility are key concerns.

By closely examining the transaction fees associated with key operations on different blockchain platforms, we gain a deeper understanding of their relative efficiency and cost-effectiveness in the context of insurance claim management. This detailed fee analysis allows us to methodically compare the capabilities and costs of platforms such as BNB Chain, Fantom, Polygon, and Celo. Our goal is to select a platform that strikes an optimal balance between operational expenses and system performance, ensuring that the blockchain solution we choose provides the necessary functionality for managing insurance claims at the most economical price. This selection process is crucial for implementing a system that not only facilitates efficient and secure processing of claims but also manages to keep the cost burden low for all entities involved, from insurance companies to claimants, thereby encouraging broader adoption and sustained use.

5 Conclusion

In this paper, we explored the integration of blockchain technology in insurance claim management, with a particular focus on RSA-encrypted NFTs and smart contracts. Our analysis indicates that blockchain can significantly improve transparency, security, and efficiency in managing insurance claims. The use of RSA-encrypted NFTs provides a secure and verifiable means of handling claim data, while smart contracts automate the process, ensuring all transactions are recorded transparently on the blockchain.

The performance evaluation demonstrated the computational demands of RSA encryption and decryption, highlighting the need for a balance between data security and processing efficiency. Furthermore, the comparative analysis of transaction fees across different EVM-compatible platforms revealed variations in cost structures, emphasizing the importance of selecting an economically viable platform for implementation.

Overall, our findings suggest that blockchain technology holds considerable promise for transforming insurance claim management. By adopting blockchain solutions, insurance companies can enhance the transparency and security of their operations, ultimately improving the efficiency of claim processing. This paper contributes to the ongoing research on blockchain applications in insurance and provides a framework for future implementations that aim to optimize claim management systems.

References

1. Abramowicz, M.: Blockchain-based insurance. George Washington University Law School (2019)
2. Alnavar, K., Babu, C.: Blockchain-based smart contract with machine learning for insurance claim verification. In: 2021 5th International Conference on Electrical, Electronics, Communication, Computer Technologies and Optimization Techniques (ICEECCOT) (2021)
3. Bang, N., et al.: Blockchain-enhanced IoHT: a patient-centric internet of healthcare things platform with smart contract-driven data management. In: Delir Haghighi, P., Khalil, I., Kotsis, G., Er, N.A.S. (eds.) MoMM 2023. LNCS, vol. 14417, pp. 50–56. Springer, Cham (2023). https://doi.org/10.1007/978-3-031-48348-6_4
4. Bhamidipati, N.R., et al.: ClaimChain: secure blockchain platform for handling insurance claims processing. IEEE (2021)
5. Bodemer, O.: Transforming the insurance industry with blockchain and smart contracts: enhancing efficiency, transparency, and trust. Eng. Open Access (2023)
6. Bordekar, J.A., Gupta, S., Tinnaluri, V., Sinha, A.: Insurance claiming process based on blockchain technology using smart contract. Int. J. Adv. Res. Ideas Innov. Technol. (2019)
7. Duong-Trung, N., et al.: On components of a patient-centered healthcare system using smart contract. In: Proceedings of the 2020 4th International Conference on Cryptography, Security and Privacy, pp. 31–35 (2020)
8. Duong-Trung, N., et al.: Smart care: integrating blockchain technology into the design of patient-centered healthcare systems. In: Proceedings of the 2020 4th International Conference on Cryptography, Security and Privacy, pp. 105–109 (2020)
9. Grishin, D., et al.: Accelerating genomic data generation and facilitating genomic data access using decentralization, privacy-preserving technologies and equitable compensation. Blockchain Healthc. Today (2018)
10. Khatun, M., Islam, R.A., Islam, S.: B-SAHIC: a blockchain based secured and automated health insurance claim processing system. J. Intell. Fuzzy Syst. (2022)
11. Le, H.T., et al.: BloodChain: a blood donation network managed by blockchain technologies. Network **2**(1), 21–35 (2022)
12. Loukil, F., Boukadi, K., Hussain, R., Abed, M.: CioSy: a collaborative blockchain-based insurance system. Electronics (2021)
13. Quynh, N.T.T., et al.: Toward a design of blood donation management by blockchain technologies. In: Gervasi, O., et al. (eds.) ICCSA 2021. LNCS, vol. 12956, pp. 78–90. Springer, Cham (2021). https://doi.org/10.1007/978-3-030-87010-2_6
14. Sawalka, S., Lahiri, A., Saveetha, D.: Ethinsurance: a blockchain based alternative approach for health insurance claim. In: 2022 International Conference on Computer Communication and Informatics (ICCCI) (2022)
15. Shinde, R., et al.: Securing AI-based healthcare systems using blockchain technology: a state-of-the-art systematic literature review and future research directions. arXiv preprint arXiv:2206.04793 (2022)
16. Thukral, M.K.: Security and efficiency in vehicle insurance: a blockchain-based solution. IEEE (2023)

17. Vo, H., Mehedy, L., Mohania, M., Abebe, E.: Blockchain-based data management and analytics for micro-insurance applications. In: Proceedings of the 2017 ACM on Conference on Information and Knowledge Management (2017)
18. Zheng, X., et al.: Blockchain-based personal health data sharing system using cloud storage. In: 2018 IEEE 20th International Conference on E-Health Networking, Applications and Services (Healthcom), pp. 1–6. IEEE (2018)

COSIS: An AI-Enabled Digital Transformation Framework Integrating Large Language Models and Key Performance Indicators

Liang-Jie Zhang[1(✉)], Huan Chen[2], Sheng He[3], Changhu Li[1], Junyang Chen[1], Haodi Zhang[1], and Wenfeng Du[1]

[1] Center for AI Services Computing, College of Computer Science and Software Engineering, Shenzhen University, Shenzhen, China
zhanglj@ieee.org
[2] SF Technology Co., Ltd., Shenzhen, China
[3] Kingdee Research, Kingdee International Software Group Co., Ltd., Shenzhen, China

Abstract. The rapid advancement of Artificial Intelligence (AI) and Large Language Models (LLMs) has significantly transformed various sectors of society, compelling enterprises to undertake comprehensive digital transformations to remain competitive in the AI era. This paper introduces COSIS, an AI-enabled digital trans-formation framework comprising five key dimensions: Culture, Operation, Strategy, Innovation, and Service. The COSIS framework provides a structured approach for enterprises to navigate the complexities of digital transformation by integrating AI and LLM technologies into their core functions. For each dimension, the paper identifies specific key performance indicators (KPIs) to measure the effectiveness of AI-enabled transformations. These KPIs enable enterprises to quantitatively assess progress and outcomes, ensuring alignment with strategic objectives and facilitating continuous improvement. Additionally, the paper discusses the implications of AI and LLM technologies on enterprise management team building in the AI era.

Keywords: Artificial Intelligence · Large Language Models · Digital Transformation · COSIS Framework · Key Performance Indicators · Enterprise Management · Culture · Operation · Strategy · Innovation · Service

1 Introduction

The rapid advancement of Artificial Intelligence (AI) and Large Language Models (LLMs) [1] has ushered in a transformative era, redefining the operational paradigms across all sectors of society [2]. These technologies have not only disrupted tradition-al business models but have also introduced innovative solutions that enhance productivity, efficiency, and competitiveness. Enterprises are increasingly recognizing the imperative to adapt to this technological evolution to maintain their relevance and drive sustainable growth.

S. He and L.-J. Zhang (Eds.): SCF/SCC 2024, LNCS 15430, pp. 74–99, 2025.
https://doi.org/10.1007/978-3-031-77000-5_6

In this new landscape of rapid technological change, there is an urgent need for a comprehensive digital transformation framework that enables organizations to navigate the complexities of integrating AI and LLM technologies into their operations. Such a framework must address the multifaceted challenges of transformation, including cultural shifts, operational realignment, strategic planning, innovation fostering, and service enhancement. Moreover, to ensure the effectiveness of the transformation process, enterprises require well-defined key performance indicators (KPIs) that align with their strategic objectives and provide measurable outcomes.

This paper introduces COSIS, an AI and Large Language Model-enabled digital transformation framework designed to guide enterprises through the intricate process of digital transformation. The COSIS framework encompasses five critical dimensions:

Culture: Fostering an organizational culture that embraces change, encourages continuous learning, and promotes a growth mindset to support AI integration.

Operation: Leveraging AI technologies to enhance operational efficiency, streamline processes, and improve customer-centric practices.

Strategy: Utilizing AI-driven analytics for strategic planning, resource optimization, and data-driven decision-making to achieve competitive advantage.

Innovation: Encouraging continuous innovation through collaborative research and development, scenario analysis, and customer-focused solutions enabled by AI.

Service: Transforming service models with AI-powered customer service, personalized experiences, and intelligent decision support systems to enhance customer satisfaction and loyalty.

For each dimension, we identify specific KPIs that enable enterprises to quantitatively assess the effectiveness of their transformation efforts. These KPIs serve as vital tools for monitoring progress, facilitating continuous improvement, and ensuring alignment with organizational goals.

The structure of this paper is organized as follows: Section 2 provides an overview of AI technologies and large language models, exploring their individual capabilities and the synergistic relationship between them. This section establishes the foundational understanding necessary for integrating these technologies into enterprise con-texts. Section 3 introduces the COSIS framework in detail, outlining its components and illustrating how AI and LLM technologies can be leveraged within each dimension. We also present the associated KPIs for measuring transformation effective-ness. Section 4 offers insights into building enterprise management teams in the AI era, emphasizing the importance of competency assessment, data-driven talent selection, performance management, collaboration, innovation incentives, and employee satisfaction. Section 5 concludes the paper by summarizing the key contributions and discussing future research directions, including the empirical validation of the COSIS framework and its long-term impacts on organizational performance.

2 Artificial Intelligence and Large Language Model

2.1 Overview of Artificial Intelligence

Artificial Intelligence is a rapidly evolving field of computer science dedicated to developing systems and machines capable of performing tasks traditionally requiring human intelligence. These tasks include learning, reasoning, problem-solving, perception, and language comprehension, utilizing advanced technologies to replicate—and in some cases, surpass—human cognitive abilities. The goal of AI goes beyond simply mimicking human thought processes; it aims to enhance and transcend them, providing solutions to complex challenges and enabling innovative interactions with technology.

The conceptual origins of AI can be traced back to the 1950s, a period marked by significant advancements in computing and theoretical frameworks. A pivotal moment in AI's history was the introduction of the Turing Test by Alan Turing in 1950. Turing proposed a thought experiment to evaluate whether a machine could exhibit intelligent behavior indistinguishable from that of a human. If a human evaluator, interacting with both a machine and a human through a text interface, could not reliably distinguish between them, the machine could be considered to possess human-level intelligence. This test laid the groundwork for future AI research, challenging scientists to develop machines capable of natural language communication and reasoning.

AI has evolved through various phases over the decades, each characterized by different approaches and levels of optimism regarding the technology's potential. Early AI research focused on symbolic AI and rule-based systems, which attempted to encode human knowledge and reasoning into explicit rules. However, these approaches faced limitations in handling the complexity and ambiguity of real-world situations.

The emergence of machine learning marked a paradigm shift by enabling computers to learn from data rather than relying solely on predefined rules. Within machine learning, deep learning has become a transformative approach. It involves neural networks with multiple layers that can learn hierarchical representations of data, significantly improving AI systems' performance in areas like image and speech recognition, natural language processing, and autonomous systems.

Several landmark achievements have demonstrated the rapid progress and capabilities of AI:

Deep Blue: Developed by IBM, Deep Blue made history in 1997 by defeating the reigning world chess champion, Garry Kasparov. This event marked the first time a computer had defeated a world champion in a standard chess tournament. Deep Blue's victory showcased AI's potential in strategic thinking and complex problem-solving, utilizing brute-force computation to assess millions of positions per second [3].

Watson: Another milestone by IBM, Watson gained prominence in 2011 when it competed on the quiz show Jeopardy! against two of the show's most successful contestants, Ken Jennings and Brad Rutter. Watson's ability to process and interpret natural language clues, access vast amounts of unstructured data, and generate accurate responses in real time highlighted significant advancements in natural language processing and information retrieval [4].

AlphaGo: Developed by DeepMind, a subsidiary of Alphabet Inc., AlphaGo achieved a groundbreaking victory in 2016 by defeating Lee Sedol, one of the world's top Go players. Go is an ancient board game known for its complexity and the vast number of possible moves, far exceeding those in chess. AlphaGo combined deep neural networks with reinforcement learning, enabling it to learn and master the game through self-play and analysis of professional games. This accomplishment underscored AI's ability to tackle problems previously deemed intractable for machines [5].

ChatGPT: Introduced by OpenAI, ChatGPT represents a significant advancement in large language models (LLMs) and conversational AI. Using the GPT (Generative Pre-trained Transformer) architecture, ChatGPT can understand and generate human-like text across various topics. It assists with tasks such as drafting emails, writing code, answering questions, and engaging in interactive dialogues. ChatGPT exemplifies the strides made in AI's ability to comprehend context, generate coherent narratives, and adapt to various conversational styles [6].

AI can be broadly categorized into two types based on the scope and capabilities of the systems:

Weak AI (Narrow AI): This category includes AI systems designed to perform specific tasks or solve particular problems. Weak AI operates under a limited set of constraints and does not possess consciousness or self-awareness. Examples include virtual personal assistants like Siri and Alexa, recommendation algorithms used by streaming services, and image recognition systems employed in medical diagnostics. These systems excel in their designated functions but cannot generalize their intelligence beyond their programmed tasks.

Strong AI (General AI): Strong AI aims to create machines with the ability to understand, learn, and apply intelligence similarly to human cognition. Such systems would be capable of performing any intellectual task that a human can, exhibiting consciousness, self-awareness, and genuine understanding. While strong AI remains a theoretical concept, it represents the ultimate goal for many AI researchers. Achieving strong AI would require significant breakthroughs in understanding consciousness and replicating the complexities of the human brain.

The continuous advancement of AI technologies has profound implications for society and industry. AI is increasingly integrated into various sectors, including healthcare, finance, transportation, and manufacturing, driving innovation and efficiency. Enterprises leverage AI to automate routine tasks, gain insights from large datasets, personalize customer experiences, and develop new products and services.

Understanding the evolution and current state of AI is crucial for organizations embarking on digital transformation initiatives. By recognizing the capabilities and limitations of AI technologies, enterprises can make informed decisions about strategically integrating AI into their operations. This integration is essential for maintaining competitiveness, fostering innovation, and enhancing operational efficiency in an increasingly digital and data-driven world.

2.2 Overview of Large Language Model

Large Language Models (LLMs) represent a significant advancement in natural language processing (NLP) and artificial intelligence. These models are deep learning-based AI systems designed to understand, generate, and manipulate human language in contextually relevant and coherent ways. The technical foundation of LLMs lies in their reliance on large-scale neural networks, particularly those based on the Transformer architecture, and their training on massive datasets comprising diverse text from the internet and other sources.

The Transformer architecture, introduced by Vaswani et al. in 2017 [7], revolutionized NLP by enabling models to capture long-range dependencies in text through mechanisms like self-attention. This architecture allows the model to weigh the significance of different words in a sentence relative to one another, improving the understanding of context and meaning. The self-attention mechanism enables the model to process input data in parallel rather than sequentially, significantly enhancing computational efficiency and scalability.

LLMs are trained using unsupervised or self-supervised learning techniques on vast amounts of textual data. This training approach allows them to learn the statistical patterns of language without explicit human annotation. Consequently, LLMs can perform a wide range of language tasks, including text completion, translation, summarization, question-answering, sentiment analysis, and even generating creative content like poetry and stories.

Prominent examples of LLMs include:

OpenAI's GPT Series: The Generative Pre-trained Transformer (GPT) models, such as GPT-3 [6], have set new benchmarks in NLP. GPT-3, with 175 billion parameters, can generate human-like text and perform tasks without explicit task-specific training, demonstrating few-shot and zero-shot learning capabilities. Its versatility has enabled applications in drafting emails, writing code, composing essays, and engaging in conversational agents. ChatGPT 4o and o1 represent a significant leap forward in conversational AI, providing a more sophisticated, contextually aware, and human-like interaction experience.

Google's BERT: Bidirectional Encoder Representations from Transformers (BERT) [8] is designed to understand the context of a word based on its surroundings (bidirectional training). BERT has significantly improved performance on various NLP tasks by providing a deeper understanding of context and nuance in language. It has been foundational in enhancing search algorithms and question-answering systems. Gemini is an advanced AI project developed by Google's DeepMind, aiming to build the next generation of AI systems that integrate cutting-edge advancements in natural language processing (NLP), reinforcement learning, and problem-solving. Announced in 2023, Gemini [9] is positioned as a major step forward in AI, designed to surpass the capabilities of existing large language models like GPT-3 and even Google's own earlier models, such as BERT.

Meta's LLaMA: Large Language Model Meta AI (LLaMA) [10] is a collection of foundation language models ranging from 8 billion to 405 billion parameters. LLaMA is trained on publicly available datasets and aims to democratize access to LLMs by being more efficient and accessible to researchers. It provides competitive performance with smaller model sizes, making it more resource-efficient and easier to deploy.

These models have been instrumental in pushing the boundaries of what AI can achieve in language understanding and generation. They have applications across numerous domains, including customer service (chatbots), content creation, coding assistance, virtual tutoring, and more.

However, the development and deployment of LLMs also present challenges. Training these models requires substantial computational resources and energy, raising concerns about environmental impact. Additionally, since they learn from data that may contain biases or misinformation, there is a risk of generating outputs that reflect these issues. Ethical considerations such as data privacy, consent, and the potential misuse of generated content are also critical factors that need to be addressed.

Despite these challenges, LLMs remain a focal point in AI research, with ongoing efforts to improve their efficiency, reduce biases, and expand their capabilities. Advancements in techniques such as model distillation, efficient training algorithms, and the use of smaller, more specialized datasets are contributing to making LLMs more accessible and sustainable.

Understanding LLMs is crucial for enterprises seeking to integrate AI into their operations. By leveraging these models, businesses can enhance communication, automate content generation, analyze large volumes of text data for insights, and create more interactive and personalized customer experiences. LLMs are a key component in the digital transformation journey, enabling organizations to harness AI's power for competitive advantage.

2.3 Relationship Between Artificial Intelligence and Large Language Model

Large Language Model is a significant subfield within Artificial Intelligence that focuses specifically on Natural Language Processing (NLP). While AI encompasses a broad spectrum of technologies aimed at replicating or enhancing human cognitive functions, Large Language Models (LLMs) concentrate on understanding and generating human language. The relationship between AI and LLMs is both complementary and synergistic, with each contributing to the advancement of the other.

LLMs represent a specialized application of AI techniques, utilizing deep learning algorithms and vast datasets to process and produce human-like text. These models leverage architectures such as the Transformer to capture complex patterns in language, enabling them to understand context, semantics, and even subtle nuances like humor or sarcasm. This specialization allows LLMs to excel in tasks such as text completion, translation, summarization, sentiment analysis, and conversational interfaces.

Other areas of AI, such as computer vision, robotics, and speech recognition, can be integrated with LLMs to enhance the overall intelligence of systems. For instance, in computer vision, combining image recognition with language models enables systems to generate descriptive captions for images or videos, improving accessibility and content understanding. In robotics, integrating LLMs allows robots to interpret verbal instructions and engage in natural language interactions, facilitating more intuitive human-robot collaboration. Speech recognition technologies paired with LLMs enhance voice-controlled applications by improving the accuracy and relevance of responses.

This interdisciplinary integration leads to the development of multimodal AI systems that can process and respond to information across different formats—text, images, audio, and video. By leveraging the strengths of various AI subfields, these systems achieve a higher level of functionality and intelligence.

Conversely, LLMs expand the scope of AI applications by enabling more natural and efficient interactions between humans and machines. Intelligent assistants like Siri,

Alexa, and Google Assistant rely on language models to understand user queries and provide relevant responses. Translation services benefit from LLMs' ability to accurately interpret and convert text between languages, breaking down communication barriers. Content generation tools utilize LLMs to produce written material for various purposes, from drafting emails and reports to creating marketing copy and even code, enhancing productivity and creativity in professional settings.

Moreover, LLMs contribute to advancements in AI by providing context-aware reasoning capabilities. They can analyze large volumes of unstructured textual data to extract insights, support decision-making processes, and personalize user experiences. This capability is particularly valuable in fields like healthcare, finance, and customer service, where understanding and responding to nuanced human communication is crucial.

The interplay between AI and Large Language Models signifies a mutual reinforcement, where advancements in one area propel progress in the other. As AI technologies continue to evolve, LLMs will play an increasingly vital role in creating intelligent systems that are more adaptable, context-aware, and capable of seamless interaction with humans. This symbiotic relationship underscores the importance of integrating LLMs into broader AI frameworks to achieve comprehensive digital transformation, drive innovation, and maintain competitiveness in various industries.

By recognizing and leveraging the complementary roles between AI and Large Language Models, organizations can develop more sophisticated and effective AI solutions. This integration not only enhances the capabilities of AI systems but also expands the possibilities for new applications, leading to improved operational efficiency and the creation of value-added services.

It is noted that the development of Large Language Models promotes the overall progress of artificial intelligence, marking a transition from quantitative to qualitative change in AI capabilities. Examples include applications in dialogue systems and sentiment analysis. The development of Large Language Models relies on large-scale datasets and powerful computational resources. In the future, it is expected that Large Language Models will be further optimized—becoming lightweight, miniaturized, and tailored to specific domains and industries—allowing AI technology to be more widely and effectively applied across various fields.

2.4 Generative AI and Ethics

In the field of image generation, generative AI has made significant contributions to computer vision. Applications such as image restoration improve image quality by filling in missing pixels or enhancing resolution. Image style transfer is another innovative application, where artistic styles are applied to images, allowing for creative transformations and novel artistic expressions. Generative Adversarial Networks (GANs) have been pivotal in producing realistic images, creating synthetic data, deepfakes, and artistic content [11]. These advancements have profound implications for fields like digital art, entertainment, and data augmentation, which is crucial for training other AI models.

Generative AI also extends to audio generation, offering applications like speech synthesis, which converts text into natural-sounding speech. This technology has improved virtual assistants and accessibility tools for visually impaired individuals. Music generation, another facet of audio generation, involves composing original music by learning patterns from existing compositions, thus assisting musicians in the creative process and providing background scores for multimedia content. Additionally, noise cancellation technologies employ generative models to remove unwanted sounds from audio recordings, enhancing clarity in communication and recordings.

In code generation, generative AI streamlines software development by providing automatic code completion tools that suggest code snippets in real-time. This capability enhances developer efficiency and reduces the likelihood of errors. Code translation, another application, involves converting code between programming languages, thereby facilitating interoperability and the modernization of legacy systems. Generative AI can also create code from natural language descriptions, aiding rapid prototyping and assisting non-programmers in bringing their ideas to life.

The advent of generative AI technologies has introduced a multitude of novel applications, prompting significant ethical considerations and legal implications. It is imperative to thoroughly examine the ethical ramifications and legal aspects associated with using technologies like sound cloning and video extension (cloning). Responsible utilization of these technologies necessitates obtaining explicit permission from the original content owners and ensuring adherence to relevant laws and regulations.

Protecting the security and privacy of users' personal data, as well as their viewing and interaction data, is paramount. Organizations must implement robust data protection measures to maintain user trust and comply with privacy laws. Additionally, there is a pressing need to remain vigilant about the Environmental, Social, and Governance (ESG) [12] impacts of new technologies. This includes assessing how technological advancements affect environmental sustainability, social equity, and corporate governance practices.

Furthermore, the potential effects of these emerging technologies on employment should not be overlooked. Integrating new technologies can lead to significant shifts in the labor market, potentially resulting in job displacement or the creation of new roles requiring different skill sets. It is essential to proactively address these changes by investing in workforce retraining and education programs to mitigate negative impacts on employment and support a smooth transition for affected workers.

3 Enhancing Enterprise Productivity: The COSIS Five-Factor Modeling Framework

To comprehensively analyze an enterprise, one might theoretically consider it across 360 dimensions. However, our research has identified five key dimensions that are particularly representative. Consequently, this paper proposes a five-factor modeling framework, termed COSIS, for constructing enterprises with enhanced productivity. The COSIS framework encompasses five elements: an enterprise's **C**ulture, **O**peration, **S**trategy, **I**nnovation, and **S**ervice. Each of these elements serves as an entry point for studying enterprise transformation. Regardless of which element one begins with, the analysis will ultimately encompass all five elements, resulting in a balanced and holistic perspective (Fig. 1).

The following sections will examine, from the perspective of the five elements of the COSIS framework, the impact that large-scale AI models will have on the five

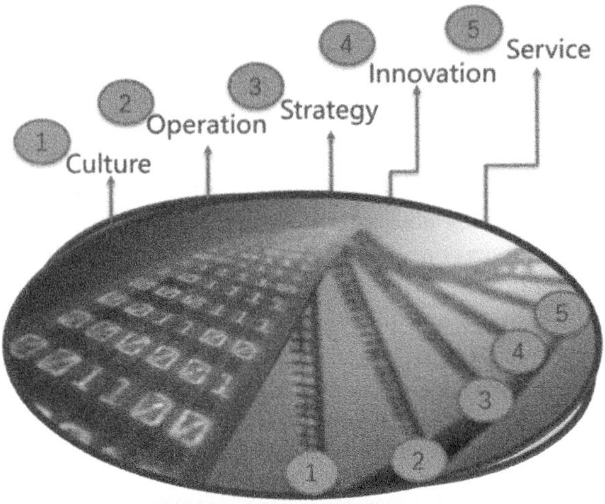

Fig. 1. COSIS model architecture diagram.

dimensions of enterprise transformation. This analysis will explore how these models can bring distinctive advancements to the future productivity of enterprises.

3.1 Culture: Harnessing AI for Cultural Transformation

A company's most important asset is not merely its employees but its corporate culture, which constitutes its core competitive advantage. Among various types of corporate cultures, the Growth Mindset plays a significant role. Proposed by Professor Carol Dweck, the Growth Mindset concept challenges static corporate cultures with rigid and unchanging organizational boundaries, advocating instead for a culture that embraces learning and adaptability [13]. The Growth Mindset posits that intelligence and abilities can be developed through effort, strategic approaches, and collaboration with others.

The importance of a Growth Mindset lies in encouraging risk-taking, stimulating innovation, enhancing employees' capacity to face challenges and change, and improving overall performance through continuous learning and improvement. Implementing a Growth Mindset involves multifaceted strategies, including providing education and training opportunities for ongoing learning, allowing employees to fail and learn from their mistakes, and fostering a culture of open and constructive feedback. By driving innovation, adapting to change, and enhancing performance, the Growth Mindset is key to long-term success.

Several prominent companies, such as Microsoft, Google, Amazon, and Nike, have successfully adopted a Growth Mindset like corporate culture. After Satya Nadella became CEO of Microsoft, the company vigorously implemented the Growth Mindset [14], emphasizing learning and cooperation, and encouraging employees to bravely experiment with new methods and innovations. As a result, Microsoft transformed into a leader in cloud computing and artificial intelligence, with significant increases in stock price and market share. Google has consistently emphasized innovation and learning by encouraging employees to continuously upgrade their skills, providing a wide range of learning resources and opportunities, and promoting learning from failure. Consequently, Google remains at the forefront of technological innovation, launching a series of impactful products and services.

Amazon's corporate culture centers around the concept of "Day 1," which means maintaining the mentality of a startup by constantly pursuing innovation and improvement. The company encourages employees to boldly try new ideas and to learn and adjust quickly from mistakes. This approach has allowed Amazon to maintain a high level of innovation and become the world's leading provider of e-commerce and cloud computing services. Nike focuses on innovation and employee development by encouraging continuous improvement and growth. The company helps employees upgrade their skills through training and development programs and creates a work environment that fosters innovation. As a result, Nike continues to hold a leading position in the global sporting goods market, consistently launching innovative products.

AI and large language models have the capability to analyze various documents within an enterprise, as well as employee feedback, to distill and communicate the core values of the organization, ensuring that the corporate culture is implemented at all levels. AI-driven chatbots powered by large language models are capable of natural language processing, enabling open, accessible, and interactive communication among employees. Furthermore, large language models can recommend training courses and resources based on employees' interests and career development needs, providing personalized learning recommendations.

The effectiveness of implementing AI in corporate culture building can be assessed through six performance indicators:

Employee Feedback and Engagement: Measure employee feedback through satisfaction surveys, and evaluate engagement by analyzing participation levels in training, innovation programs, and other growth opportunities.

Learning and Development: Assess the percentage of employees who have completed training programs, and evaluate improvements in skills and knowledge through assessments and evaluations.

Innovation and Improvement: Track the number of new products or services introduced within a specific period and evaluate the number of patents and innovations obtained.

Performance Metrics: Incorporate growth and learning indicators into employee performance appraisals, and observe the organization's financial performance after implementing the Growth Mindset, including revenue growth and profitability improvements.

Adaptability: Analyze the company's responsiveness and flexibility in the face of market changes and challenges. Monitor whether employee turnover rates have decreased and retention rates have increased.

Number of Successful Cases: Evaluate the organization's ability to learn from mistakes by counting the number of specific successful cases after implementing the Growth Mindset.

As a proof of concept shown in Fig. 2, we developed a GPT titled *COSIS AI Enterprise* [15] in the GPT Store, incorporating the contents introduced in this paper.

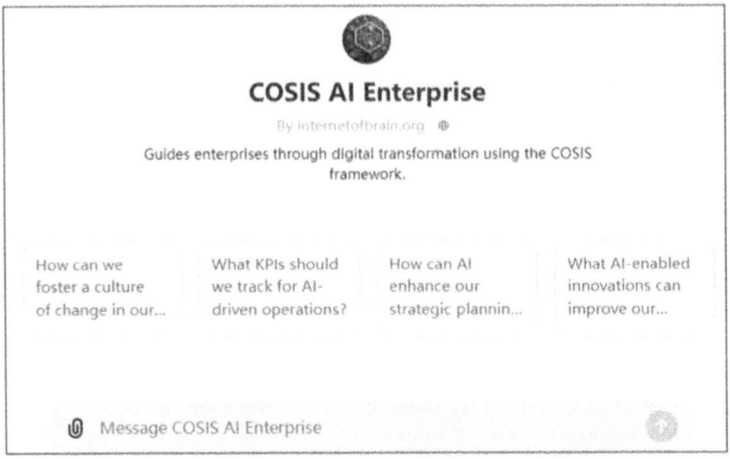

Fig. 2. COSIS AI Enterprise in the GPT Store

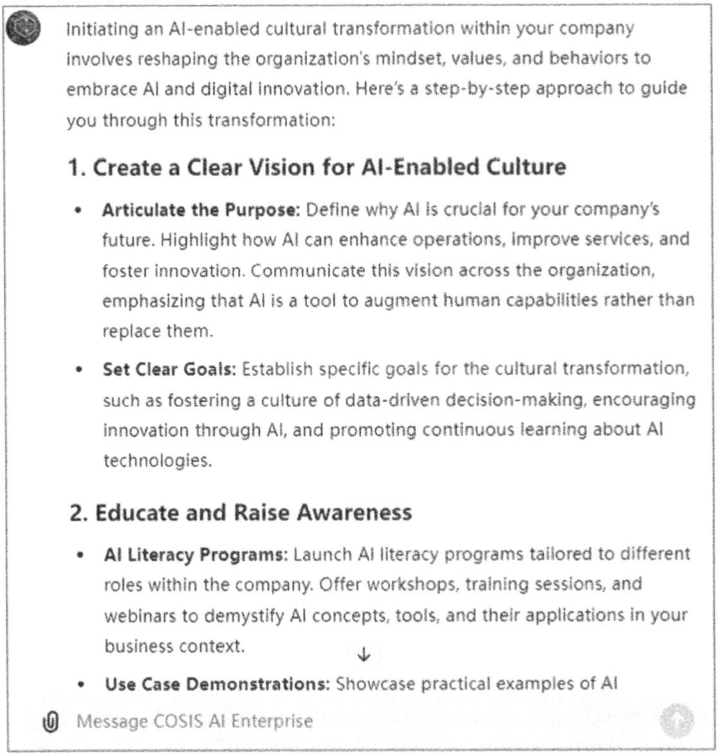

Fig. 3. Responses from *COSIS AI Enterprise* on cultural transformation.

An example prompt for COSIS AI Enterprise is: "I run an education service company that provides IT infrastructure development, course creation, and delivery for universities. How can I initiate an AI-enabled cultural transformation within my company?" The responses from *COSIS AI Enterprise* are illustrated in Fig. 3.

By focusing on these indicators, organizations can quantitatively and qualitatively assess the impact of AI and the Growth Mindset on their corporate culture, leading to sustained innovation and competitive advantage.

3.2 Operations: Utilizing AI for Operational Transformation

Operational change is not merely a process of reengineering aimed at improving efficiency. Effective operational change also requires a commitment to customer-centricity, obtaining customer feedback, and gaining insights into the industry market.

For example, in online game operations, in-game voice communication can sometimes involve inappropriate speech from players, which seriously affects the game ecosystem and operational environment. To address this issue, Modulate has developed ToxMod [16], the first active voice chat monitoring system specifically designed for games. Based on advanced machine learning technology, this system can classify players' voice chat signals, analyze conversation details to determine toxicity (i.e., alignment with social norms and environmental expectations), flag undesirable speech behaviors, and provide administrators with relevant and accurate context to expedite incident responses. This ensures player safety and privacy while purifying the environment of the game operation or platform.

Another pertinent example is the rapidly changing market dynamics in today's industry, which necessitate swift responses to market feedback and demand. New products or services often need to be advertised promptly. AI-generated content (AIGC) can create high-quality video content or poster rapidly, enabling companies to respond quickly to market feedback and demand. To promote the micro-drama "White Moonlight: AI Dream Factory," we used ChatGPT 4o to generate a promotional poster shown in Fig. 4.

Fig. 4. AI-generated poster for the micro-drama

This AI-generated poster for the micro-drama "White Moonlight: AI Dream Factory" features a futuristic, industrial landscape dominated by a massive, glowing moon-like orb hovering above a high-tech facility. The facility is equipped with advanced robotic arms and machinery, suggesting a futuristic factory or laboratory. The surrounding environment is dark and illuminated by the blue and white glow emanating from the moon and the various parts of the facility, creating an ethereal and otherworldly atmosphere. In the background, a starry sky with a faint Milky Way adds a cosmic, dreamlike quality to the scene, emphasizing the blend of technology and fantasy central to the micro-drama's theme.

Artificial intelligence and large language models can analyze and forecast market data, monitor market trends in real time, predict changes in demand, and enhance market responsiveness. Regarding customer feedback, AI-driven customer feedback systems can analyze input in real time using voice recognition and sentiment analysis technologies, allowing for rapid responses to customer needs.

In terms of process optimization, AI and large models can be employed for process mining and optimization, automatically identifying and improving bottlenecks in business processes, thereby enhancing process agility and efficiency.

Enterprises need to recalibrate assessment indicators to support operational changes following each transformation. The effect of AI implementation on business operations can be assessed in four aspects: market insights, customer feedback, process optimization, and comprehensive metrics.

Market Insights

The effectiveness of AI implementation in market insights can be assessed using four metrics: *Market Response Time*: Measures how quickly a company can react to market changes and trends; a shorter response time indicates better adaptability. *Prediction Accuracy*: Assesses the accuracy of market demand forecasting by comparing predictions with actual outcomes, thus evaluating the reliability of AI models. *Sales Growth Rate*: Observes the increase in sales following market insights, especially during periods of market fluctuation, to determine the impact on revenue. *Market Share Change*: Evaluates the increase in competitiveness resulting from market insights by regularly monitoring changes in market share.

Customer Feedback

Similarly, four metrics can be used to assess the effectiveness of AI implementation in handling customer feedback: *Customer Satisfaction*: Measures satisfaction with the speed and quality of feedback response through customer satisfaction surveys and Net Promoter Score (NPS) scores. *Response Time*: Assesses the average time between receiving customer feedback and providing a solution, indicating efficiency in addressing customer needs. *Sentiment Analysis Accuracy*: Evaluates the accuracy of sentiment analysis by comparing AI-generated results with actual customer sentiment, ensuring reliable interpretations. *Customer Retention:* Observes retention rates after feedback, particularly following the resolution of negative feedback, to assess loyalty and satisfaction.

Process Optimization

The effectiveness of operational changes in process optimization can be assessed using the following four metrics: *Process Efficiency:* Measures the execution time of optimized business processes; shorter execution times reflect improved efficiency. *Cost Savings:* Calculates savings in human resources, materials, and time achieved through process optimization, reflecting financial benefits. *Bottleneck Reduction Number:* Assesses the number of process bottlenecks identified and resolved by the AI model, indicating improvements in workflow. *Productivity Improvement:* Observes changes in the productivity of employees or production units after process optimization, highlighting enhancements in output.

Comprehensive Metrics

In addition to the specific assessment metrics for the previous areas, the following overall metrics provide a comprehensive evaluation of enterprise performance after AI-enabled operations: *Overall Profitability:* Assesses changes in the overall profitability of the enterprise following the implementation of AI-enabled operations, indicating financial health. *Return on Investment (ROI):* Calculates the ratio of AI technology investment to the revenue gained, measuring the economic benefits and justifying the investment. *Competitive Advantage:* Evaluates the organization's competitive edge through its overall performance in market position, innovation capability, and customer satisfaction.

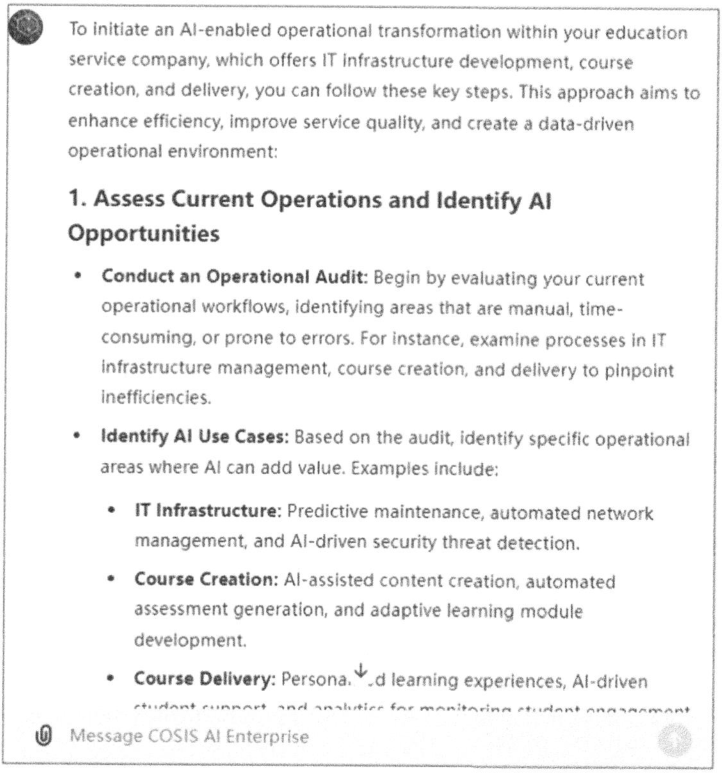

Fig. 5. Responses from COSIS AI Enterprise on operational transformation.

By utilizing these metrics, organizations can quantitatively and qualitatively assess the impact of AI on operational changes, supporting continuous improvement and strategic decision-making. The integration of AI technologies, particularly large models, plays a crucial role in enhancing market responsiveness, improving customer interactions, and optimizing processes, ultimately contributing to sustained competitive advantage.

Next, we explore operational transformation. The prompt: "How can I initiate an AI-enabled operational transformation within my company?" leads to responses from *COSIS AI Enterprise*, which are presented in Fig. 5.

3.3 Strategy: Empowering Strategic Transformation Through AI

The third major new qualitative productivity aspect of business change is strategic transformation or what can also be called strategic change. Strategy development requires systematic strategic grooming, using large language models for business and opportunity gap analysis, identifying innovation focuses, developing specific strategic initiatives, and optimizing strategic planning through data-driven simulation and forecasting. In addition, strategic planning must emphasize resource integration, use large language models for resource integration and optimization, and analyze online and offline data to improve resource allocation efficiency. Moreover, it is important to fully consider the role of data elements in the strategic upgrading of the enterprise, complete the data-driven, implement a data analysis platform driven by large language models, use user behavior data for personalized recommendations, optimize products and services, and create new business models.

When doing systematic strategy grooming, it is fully capable of integrating methodologies into the AI model to improve efficiency, expand thinking and stimulate innovation. For example, expanding IBM's Business Leadership Model (BLM) [17] to integrate AI and Large Language Models (LLMs) like GPT-4 involves enhancing both strategic planning and execution through AI-driven insights and automation. The diagram shown in Fig. 6 illustrates how AI can be incorporated into key strategic and execution components to create a cohesive and adaptive leadership model.

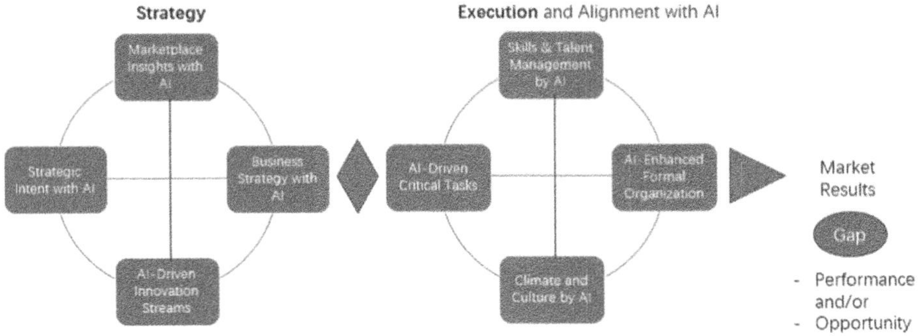

Fig. 6. AI-Driven Business Leadership Model for adaptively aligning strategy and execution

On the strategy side, "Marketplace Insights with AI" uses AI tools to gather and analyze large-scale market data, offering real-time insights into customer preferences, competitive landscape, and emerging trends. This data-driven approach informs "Strategic Intent with AI," allowing leaders to define clear, adaptable goals aligned with the latest market conditions. The "Business Strategy with AI" component leverages LLMs to model different strategic scenarios, optimize decision-making, and enable data-driven strategy formulation. This strategic layer is completed by "AI-Driven Innovation Streams," where AI accelerates the ideation process, identifies opportunities for innovation, and prioritizes projects that offer the highest value. By continuously iterating on these strategic components, companies can maintain an agile and forward-looking approach to their business strategies.

On the execution and alignment side, the diagram emphasizes "AI-Driven Critical Tasks," where AI automates routine operational tasks, enhancing efficiency and freeing up human resources for more complex, strategic initiatives. "Skills & Talent Management by AI" involves using AI to identify skill gaps, personalize employee learning paths, and ensure that the workforce remains equipped to support AI-driven operations. The "AI-Enhanced Formal Organization" component employs AI to optimize organizational structure, streamline workflows, and facilitate communication and collaboration across different departments. Finally, "Climate and Culture by AI" leverages AI to monitor and influence organizational culture, promoting inclusivity, ethical behavior, and a climate that supports continuous learning and adaptation.

The diagram's flow culminates in "Market Results," with AI helping to identify and address performance gaps. By closing the loop between strategy and execution, AI enables organizations to continuously measure and refine their approach, ensuring that strategic planning and operational execution remain aligned. This integrated model not only drives efficiency and innovation but also enables businesses to adapt swiftly to changing market dynamics, maintaining a competitive edge in the AI era.

The effective application of AI and large language models can not only help streamline organizational processes but also expedite strategic planning and potentially drive business model innovation. LLMs can be used to construct personalized recommendation systems. For example, e-commerce platforms utilize AI models to analyze user behavior, offer personalized product recommendations, and enhance user engagement and sales. Netflix and Amazon are prominent examples of this application. Additionally, LLMs can be employed for content creation, automatically generating high-quality articles, advertisements, video scripts, and more, thus enabling companies to quickly produce and disseminate content. OpenAI's GPT series is widely recognized for its effectiveness in content generation. AI models also assist in the development of smart products, including smart hardware and software, such as voice assistants (e.g., Alexa and Siri) and smart home systems, thereby enhancing the overall user experience.

Post-AI-enabled strategic planning or strategic management allows enterprises to evaluate performance changes and measure the benefits of strategic transformation through various performance indicators, including systematic strategy formulation, resource integration, data-driven decision-making, and comprehensive metrics.

Systematic Strategy Formulation can be assessed using the following metrics: *Strategy Formulation Efficiency*: Measures the reduction in time for strategic planning through AI technology compared to traditional methods. *Number of Innovation Projects:* Counts the new innovation projects identified and launched with AI assistance. *Strategy*

Achievement Rate: Evaluates the realization of strategic goals, including the completion rate of key performance indicators (KPIs). *Simulation Prediction Accuracy*: Assesses the accuracy of AI simulation predictions by comparing them with actual outcomes.

Resource Integration can be evaluated through: *Resource Utilization*: Measures the effectiveness of resource allocation, including human, material, and financial resources. *Cost Savings*: Calculates cost reductions following resource optimization, including savings in labor and inventory costs. *Efficiency Improvement*: Assesses operational efficiency gains post-resource integration, such as reduced production cycles and faster delivery. *Reduction of Resource Conflicts*: Quantifies the reduction of conflicts or redundancies in resource allocation to ensure a more rational distribution.

Data-Driven Decision Making is assessed using: *User Conversion Rate*: Evaluates the conversion rate and sales improvement after personalized recommendations. *User Satisfaction*: Measures satisfaction following personalized recommendations and product optimization through surveys and NPS scores. *Success Rate of New Business Models*: Assesses the success and market acceptance of new data-driven business models. *Data Analysis Accuracy*: Compares the accuracy of data analytics predictions with actual business performance.

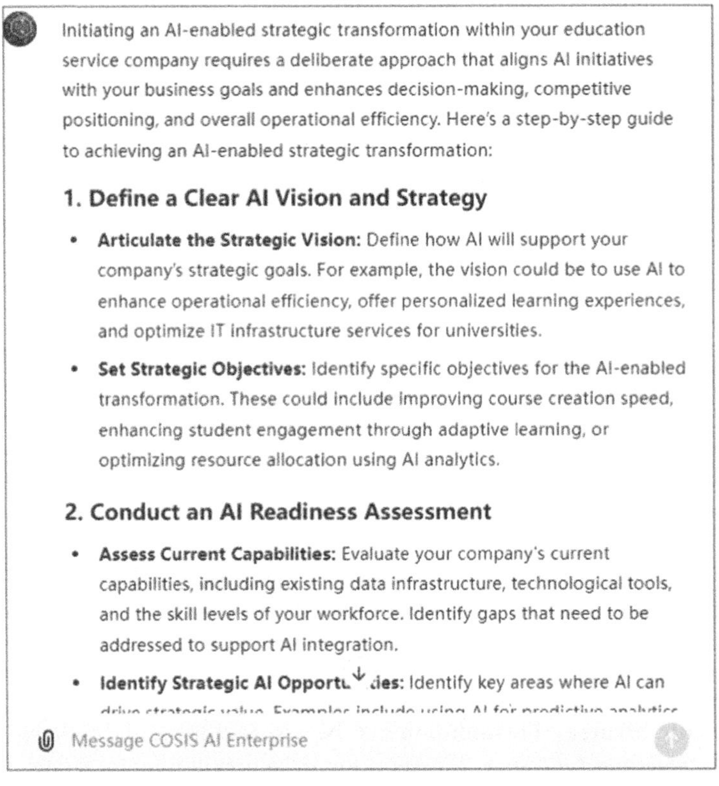

Fig. 7. Responses from COSIS AI Enterprise on strategic transformation.

Comprehensive Metrics for assessing overall enterprise performance after AI-enabled strategies include: *Strategy Execution Rate (SER)*: Measures the implementation and fulfillment of overall strategic goals. *Return on Investment (ROI)*: Calculates the ratio of AI technology investment to the returns after strategy implementation, assessing economic benefits. *Market Competitiveness*: Assesses the organization's market competitiveness based on market share, brand value, and customer loyalty. *Business Growth Rate*: Observes business growth post-AI strategy implementation, including revenue growth and profit improvements.

For strategic transformation, the prompt: "How can I initiate an AI-enabled strategic transformation within my company?" produces responses from *COSIS AI Enterprise*, as shown in Fig. 7. By systematically employing these metrics, enterprises can comprehensively assess the effectiveness of AI-enabled strategic transformation, guiding ongoing strategic planning and enhancing overall business performance. The integration of AI and large language models into strategic planning processes enables data-driven insights, resource optimization, and personalized decision-making, thereby fostering innovation and sustainable competitive advantage.

3.4 Innovation: Driving Innovation Transformation with AI

Innovation represents the fourth element of enhanced productivity and is a continuous process essential for maintaining competitiveness. Companies that fail to innovate risk losing their market position and may not sustain success in the long term. Artificial intelligence and large models facilitate innovation across three primary dimensions:

Collaborative R&D Dimension: Utilizing large model-driven collaborative research and development (R&D) platforms to achieve cross-departmental and cross-organizational innovation, thereby accelerating the product development cycle.

Scenario-Driven Dimension: Employing large models to analyze business scenarios within industries and sectors, identifying potential needs and driving product and service innovation.

Customer-Centric Dimension: Leveraging large models to analyze customer data and provide personalized solutions, enhancing customer satisfaction and loyalty.

Large models can drive product innovation, as demonstrated by advancements in sound cloning technology. This technology allows users to edit and organize audio and video content with the ease of editing text documents in word processors like Microsoft Word, particularly when producing live online audio content.

For instance, Descript's Overdub [18] utilizes text to generate speech, perform sound editing and correction, and enables multi-channel podcast production, video editing, and Studio Sound denoising. Similarly, iSpeech [19] offers text-to-speech and speech-to-text capabilities, allowing the creation of custom sound models for synthesizing specific vocals. Moreover, Resemble AI [20] provides tools to create customized sound clones, generating realistic synthesized speech suitable for developers to integrate into applications via API.

Another aspect of large model-driven business scenario innovation is the reconfiguration facilitated by **AI Agents**. An AI Agent is an intelligent robot that handles business tasks within each segment of a business process, with these intelligent robots being unified and coordinated by collaborative management systems.

For example, Fig. 8 describes how AI and large language models can be used to reconstruct business scenarios through various AI agents to handle and optimize different business processes.

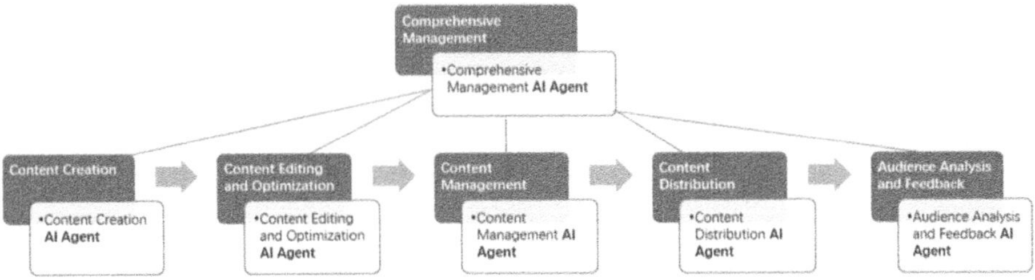

Fig. 8. Business scenario-driven innovation using AI Agents

The business process begins with Content Creation, managed by the Content Creation AI Agent. This agent is responsible for generating new content, whether it be text, audio, video, or other media forms. The focus here is on leveraging AI to produce high-quality content that aligns with the organization's objectives and audience needs.

Following content creation is the Content Editing and Optimization stage, handled by the Content Editing and Optimization AI Agent. This stage involves refining the generated content to enhance its quality and effectiveness. The AI agent optimizes the content by making adjustments, improving language use, and ensuring the content is ready for distribution. This process is crucial for maintaining a high standard of content quality.

Next is the Content Management stage, where the Content Management AI Agent takes over. This agent manages the organized storage, retrieval, and overall handling of content. It ensures that content is systematically archived and accessible, streamlining workflows and facilitating efficient content usage. Effective content management is essential for maintaining an organized content repository that can be easily utilized for future projects.

The Content Distribution stage is managed by the Content Distribution AI Agent. This stage focuses on disseminating the content through various channels to reach the target audience effectively. The AI agent determines the most appropriate distribution methods and channels, such as social media, websites, or email campaigns, to maximize content visibility and engagement.

Finally, the Audience Analysis and Feedback stage involves the Audience Analysis and Feedback AI Agent. This agent collects and analyzes audience feedback to inform future content strategies. By leveraging AI to understand audience preferences and responses, the organization can tailor its content more effectively, ensuring it meets the audience's needs and enhances overall engagement.

All these stages are interconnected and coordinated under the overarching Comprehensive Management AI Agent. This central AI agent ensures a seamless flow of content from creation to feedback, optimizing the entire content lifecycle. The framework illustrates an AI-driven end-to-end content management system aimed at enhancing the efficiency and effectiveness of content creation, distribution, and audience engagement.

Evaluating the effectiveness of AI-enabled innovation can be conducted using various performance indicators across the collaborative R&D dimension, scenario-driven dimension, customer-centric dimension, and comprehensive metrics.

From **Collaborative R&D Perspective**, the evaluation metrics include: *Reduction in Product Development Cycle Time*: Measures the decrease in time taken for products to move from concept to market with the assistance of AI. *Efficiency of Cross-Departmental Cooperation*: Assesses the effectiveness of cross-departmental and cross-organizational collaborative R&D, including project completion time and the degree of team collaboration. *Number of Innovation Projects*: Counts the number of innovation projects initiated and completed through the collaborative R&D platform. *R&D Cost Savings*: Evaluates the reduction in R&D costs, including labor and material expenses, achieved through the collaborative R&D platform.

From **Scenario-Driven Perspective**, the evaluation metrics include: *Number of New Products/Services*: Measures the number of new products or services identified and launched through scenario analysis. *Market Demand Match*: Assesses how well the new product or service aligns with market demand, verified through market research and sales data. *Market Share*: Observes the share and acceptance of new products or services in the target market. *Innovation Success Rate*: Evaluates the success rate of scenario-driven innovation projects, reflecting the accuracy of identifying potential demand.

From **Customer-Centric Perspective**, the evaluation indicators include: *Customer Satisfaction*: Measures customer satisfaction with personalized solutions through surveys and Net Promoter Score (NPS) assessments. *Customer Loyalty*: Evaluates improvements in customer loyalty, including repeat purchase rates and customer retention rates. *Effectiveness of Personalized Recommendations*: Measures sales growth and user conversions following personalized recommendations. *Customer Problem Resolution Rate*: Assesses the efficiency of quickly responding to and resolving customer problems through personalized solutions.

Some Comprehensive Metrics are used to comprehensively assess the impact on business development and performance after AI-enabled innovation. The following overall indicators can be considered: *Return on Innovation Investment (ROII)*: Calculates the ratio of AI technology investment to the revenue generated by the innovation results, measuring the economic benefits of the innovation investment. *Market Competitiveness*: Assesses the company's competitiveness in the post-innovation market through performance metrics such as market share, brand value, and technological leadership. *Business Growth Rate*: Observes business growth following the implementation of AI-enabled innovation, including revenue growth and profit improvement. *Number of Intellectual Property Rights and Patents*: Evaluates the intellectual property rights and patents applied for and obtained after AI-enabled innovation as a reflection of the innovation outcomes.

By systematically applying these metrics, organizations can quantitatively and qualitatively assess the effectiveness of AI-enabled innovation initiatives. The integration of AI and large language models into innovation processes facilitates collaborative development, scenario analysis, and customer-centric solutions, thereby fostering sustained competitive advantage and driving business growth.

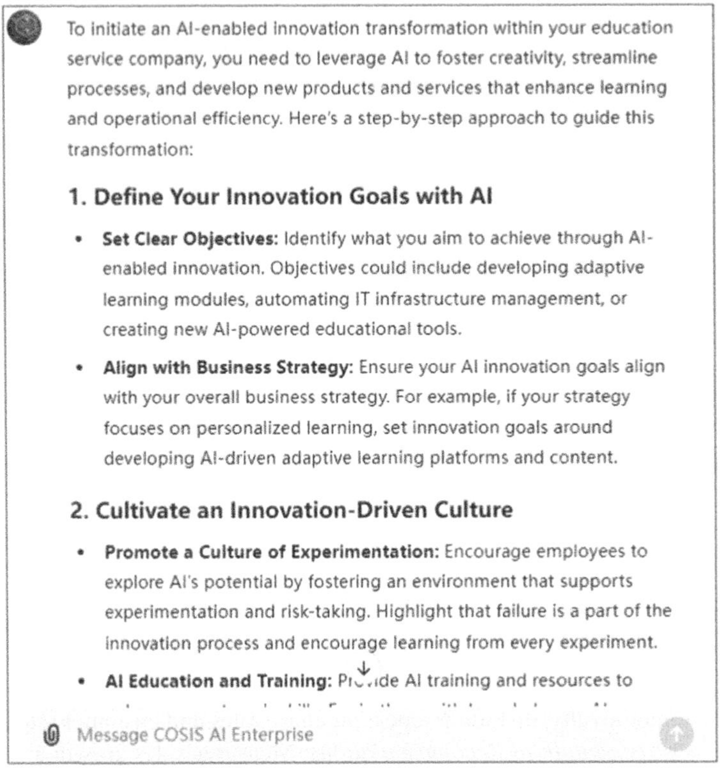

Fig. 9. Responses from COSIS AI Enterprise on innovation transformation.

Regarding innovation transformation, the prompt: "How can I initiate an AI-enabled innovation transformation within my company?" results in responses from *COSIS AI Enterprise*, presented in Fig. 9.

3.5 Service: Revolutionizing Enterprise Services Through AI

The final dimension of new quality productivity is Service, which, in this context, refers not to traditional after-sales service but to a novel model of service transformation. This section discusses the transformation of modern enterprises in the service dimension from three perspectives:

Service-Oriented Transformation: Utilizing intelligent customer service, product/resource as a service, and after-sales service platforms driven by AI and large language models to improve service efficiency and promote the shift of enterprises from product-oriented to service-oriented models.

Customer Experience Enhancement: Emphasizing comprehensive analysis of customer usage behaviors, optimizing customer journeys, and improving customer experience through AI and large language models as well as big data technologies.

Trusted Advisor: Building intelligent decision support systems driven by AI and large language models to provide customers with personalized and accurate solutions, becoming a trusted long-term partner for customers, and facilitating customer success.

Artificial intelligence is poised to bring significant changes to the future service industry and the way organizations interact with customers. When an organization introduces AI for service transformation, the effectiveness of this transformation can be evaluated using five refined metrics: *Customer Service Response Time*: Measures the reduction in average response time achieved by intelligent customer service systems. *Customer Service Completion Rate*: Assesses the number and rate of customer requests completed through intelligent customer service systems. *Customer Satisfaction*: Evaluates customer satisfaction with service quality through customer satisfaction surveys and Net Promoter Score (NPS) assessments. *Degree of Service Cost Reduction*: Calculates the reduction in service costs achieved through intelligent customer service and after-sales service platforms, including labor and operating costs. *Service Revenue Ratio*: Measures the change in the proportion of service revenue in total revenue, reflecting the success of the transition from product-based to service-based models.

In customer service, enhancing the customer experience is critical. The transformative impact of AI on customer experience can be assessed through the following five metrics: *Customer Retention Rate:* Measures improvements in customer retention after optimizing the customer journey. *Customer Experience Scores:* Obtains customer ratings and feedback on the overall experience through customer experience surveys. *Customer Complaint Rate:* Monitors changes in the number and rate of customer complaints, assessing improvements in customer satisfaction. *Accuracy of Usage Behavior Analysis:* Assesses the accuracy of the AI model in analyzing customer usage behavior by comparing actual behavior with analysis results. *Effectiveness of Personalized Recommendations:* Evaluated by customer engagement and sales growth after optimizing the customer journey and providing personalized recommendations.

From the perspective of becoming a Trusted Advisor, the following five evaluation metrics are established: *Customer Conversion Rate*: Measures the increase in customer conversion rates and sales enhancement after implementing solutions provided by the intelligent decision support system. *Customer Feedback and Satisfaction*: Evaluates customer satisfaction with the advice and solutions provided by the intelligent decision support system. *Customer Success Cases*: Counts the number of specific cases where customers have achieved success with the help of intelligent decision support systems. *Number of Long-Term Cooperative Customers*: Assesses the effectiveness of intelligent decision support systems in enhancing customer loyalty and establishing long-term cooperative relationships. *Solution Accuracy*: Assesses the accuracy and effectiveness of the solutions by comparing actual results with the recommendations provided by the intelligent decision support system.

To comprehensively assess business performance after implementing AI-enabled services, the following overall indicators can also be considered: *Overall Profitability*: Assesses changes in overall profitability following the implementation of AI-enabled services. *Return on Investment (ROI)*: Calculates the ratio of AI technology investment to the revenue gained from service improvements, measuring the economic benefits of the investment. *Market Competitiveness*: Evaluates the company's competitiveness through comprehensive performance indicators such as market share, brand value, and customer satisfaction. *Business Growth Rate*: Observes business growth after the implementation of AI-enabled services, including revenue growth and profit improvements.

By focusing on these dimensions and metrics, enterprises can effectively transform their service models through AI, leading to enhanced productivity, improved customer satisfaction, and sustained competitive advantage in the marketplace.

To focus on service transformation, the prompt: "How can I initiate an AI-enabled service transformation within my company?" generates responses from *COSIS AI Enterprise*, displayed in Fig. 10.

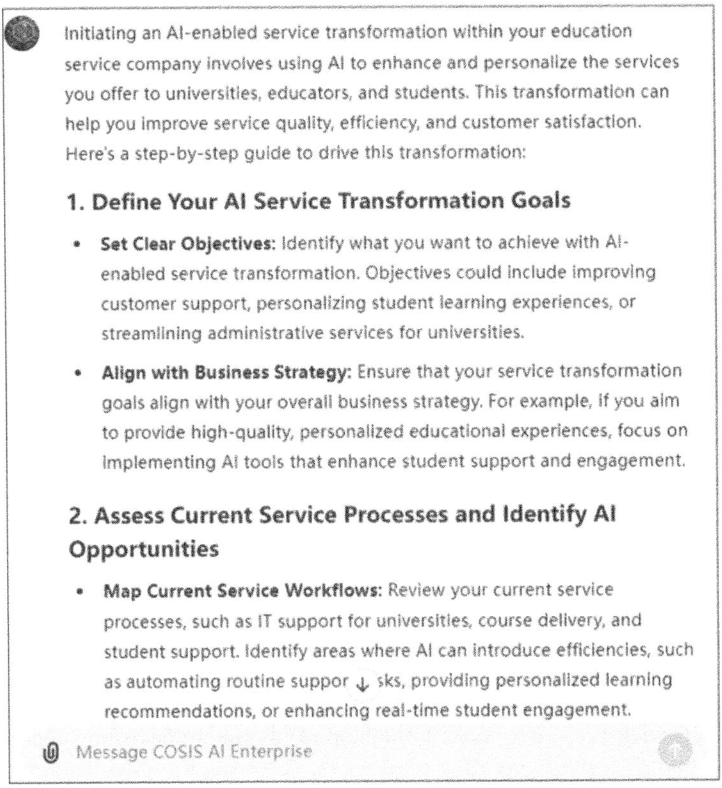

Initiating an AI-enabled service transformation within your education service company involves using AI to enhance and personalize the services you offer to universities, educators, and students. This transformation can help you improve service quality, efficiency, and customer satisfaction. Here's a step-by-step guide to drive this transformation:

1. Define Your AI Service Transformation Goals

- **Set Clear Objectives:** Identify what you want to achieve with AI-enabled service transformation. Objectives could include improving customer support, personalizing student learning experiences, or streamlining administrative services for universities.
- **Align with Business Strategy:** Ensure that your service transformation goals align with your overall business strategy. For example, if you aim to provide high-quality, personalized educational experiences, focus on implementing AI tools that enhance student support and engagement.

2. Assess Current Service Processes and Identify AI Opportunities

- **Map Current Service Workflows:** Review your current service processes, such as IT support for universities, course delivery, and student support. Identify areas where AI can introduce efficiencies, such as automating routine suppor ↓ sks, providing personalized learning recommendations, or enhancing real-time student engagement.

Fig. 10. Responses from COSIS AI Enterprise on service transformation.

4 Leadership Team Building in the Age of Artificial Intelligence

The digital transformation framework based on artificial intelligence and large language models, along with its key performance indicators constructed in this paper, offers significant insights and implications for the development of enterprise management teams in the AI era.

In terms of competency assessment and development, large-scale AI models can be utilized to construct competency assessment frameworks that evaluate the abilities and potential of management personnel. Based on the assessment results, personalized training and development plans can be formulated to address specific skill gaps and enhance overall competency within the management team.

Regarding data-driven selection, individuals with leadership potential can be identified through big data analysis. Comprehensive assessments combining historical performance data with current performance metrics enable organizations to make informed decisions when selecting candidates for managerial positions.

In the area of continuous performance management, AI-based real-time feedback mechanisms can be established to promote ongoing improvement among managers. Goals and tasks can be dynamically adjusted based on real-time data analytics, ensuring alignment with organizational objectives and responsiveness to changing conditions. For cross-departmental collaboration, AI-driven collaboration platforms can facilitate enhanced communication and cooperation among management teams across different departments. Implementing knowledge-sharing mechanisms can improve the collective capabilities of managers, fostering a more integrated and efficient organizational environment.

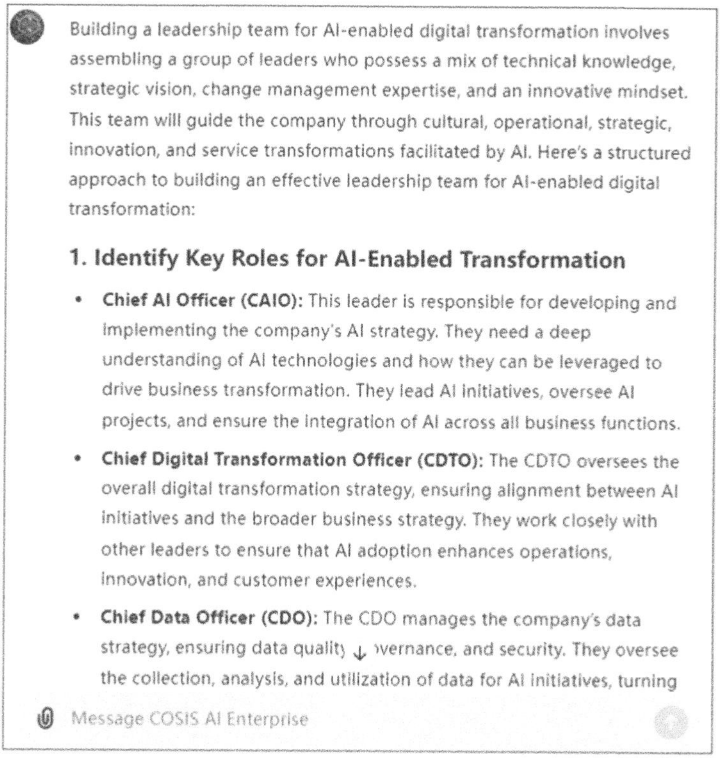

Fig. 11. Responses from COSIS AI Enterprise on building a leadership team.

Concerning innovation incentive mechanisms, AI-driven reward systems can assess and incentivize innovative performance among managers. By integrating these systems with data analytics, organizations can formulate diversified incentive structures that stimulate enthusiasm and drive for innovation within the management team.

In terms of employee satisfaction enhancement, AI technologies can be employed to conduct sentiment analysis to promptly understand the work status and psychological needs of managers. Based on the analysis results, employee support programs can be developed to enhance satisfaction and loyalty, contributing to a more motivated and committed management team.

To address leadership development, the prompt: "How can I build a leadership team for this AI-enabled digital transformation?" generates responses from *COSIS AI Enterprise*, which are shown in Fig. 11. Overall, the integration of artificial intelligence and large language models into leadership team building presents numerous opportunities for improving competency assessment, talent selection, performance management, collaboration, innovation incentives, and employee satisfaction. These advancements are critical for organizations aiming to thrive in the rapidly evolving AI era.

5 Conclusions and Future Directions

This paper has examined the domains of artificial intelligence, large language models, and generative AI application technologies, analyzing their significant impact on modern enterprises. Through this exploration, we argue that enterprises across all sectors need to pursue innovation and breakthroughs to undertake a new form of digital transformation. Such transformation is essential for developing into AI-era enterprises characterized by enhanced productivity and competitiveness.

We have proposed a digital transformation framework encompassing five key dimensions: Culture, Operation, Strategy, Innovation, and Service (COSIS), leveraging AI and large language models, along with associated key performance indicators (KPIs). The COSIS framework serves as a comprehensive guide for enterprises pursuing digital transformation in the AI era. By offering a diverse set of KPIs, the framework enables enterprises to more accurately assess the effectiveness of their transformation efforts.

The initial implementation of the COSIS framework has been developed in the GPT Store as *COSIS AI Enterprise*, presenting numerous opportunities for future research and practical application. As highlighted in [21], future studies could focus on empirically validating the framework across diverse industries and organizational sizes to assess its adaptability and effectiveness. Additionally, exploring the long-term impacts of AI-driven digital transformation on organizational culture, employee engagement, and customer satisfaction would offer valuable insights. Developing case studies and best practices based on the COSIS framework could further aid enterprises in successfully navigating the complexities of digital transformation in the AI era.

References

1. Brown, T., et al.: Language models are few-shot learners. In: Advances in Neural Information Processing Systems, vol. 33, pp. 1877–1901 (2020). https://doi.org/10.48550/arXiv.2005.14165
2. Al-Mekhlal, M., Al-Buraik, M., Al-Lubli, M.: Digital transformation: AI-powered bot solutions and automation for customer services. In: 2023 International Conference on Digital Applications, Transformation & Economy (ICDATE), Miri, Sarawak, Malaysia, pp. 1–7 (2023). https://doi.org/10.1109/ICDATE58146.2023.10248458
3. Campbell, M., Hoane, A.J., Hsu, F.-H.: Deep blue. Artif. Intell. **134**(1–2), 57–83 (2002). https://doi.org/10.1016/S0004-3702(01)00129-1
4. Ferrucci, D., et al.: Building watson: an overview of the DeepQA project. AI Mag. **31**(3), 59–79 (2010). https://doi.org/10.1609/aimag.v31i3.2303
5. Silver, D., et al.: Mastering the game of Go with deep neural networks and tree search. Nature **529**(7587), 484–489 (2016). https://doi.org/10.1038/nature16961
6. OpenAI: GPT-4. https://chatgpt.com/. Accessed 10 Sept 2024
7. Vaswani, A., et al.: Attention is all you need. In: Advances in Neural Information Processing Systems, vol. 30, pp. 5998–6008 (2017). https://doi.org/10.48550/arXiv.1706.03762
8. Devlin, J., Chang, M.-W., Lee, K., Toutanova, K.: BERT: pre-training of deep bidirectional transformers for language understanding. In: Proceedings of the 2019 Conference of the North American Chapter of the Association for Computational Linguistics: Human Language Technologies, vol. 1, pp. 4171–4186 (2019). https://doi.org/10.48550/arXiv.1810.04805
9. Google: Gemini. https://gemini.google.com/. Accessed 1 Sept 2024
10. Touvron, H., et al.: LLaMA: open and efficient foundation language models. arXiv preprint arXiv:2302.13971 (2023). https://doi.org/10.48550/arXiv.2302.13971
11. Goodfellow, I., et al.: Generative adversarial nets. In: Advances in Neural Information Processing Systems, vol. 27, pp. 2672–2680 (2014). https://doi.org/10.48550/arXiv.1406.2661
12. Eccles, R.G., Ioannou, I., Serafeim, G.: The impact of corporate sustainability on organizational processes and performance. Manage. Sci. **60**(11), 2835–2857 (2014). https://doi.org/10.1287/mnsc.2014.1984
13. Dweck, C.S., Yeager, D.S.: Mindsets: a view from two eras. Perspect. Psychol. Sci. **14**(3), 481–496 (2019). https://doi.org/10.1177/1745691618804166
14. Hogan, K., Warrenfeltz, R.: How microsoft uses a growth mindset to develop leaders. Harvard Bus. Rev. (2016). https://hbr.org/2016/10/how-microsoft-uses-a-growth-mindset-to-develop-leaders. Accessed 1 Sept 2024
15. COSIS AI Enterprise. https://chatgpt.com/g/g-yrGj0UkMv-cosis-ai-enterprise. Accessed 1 Sept 2024
16. Modulate: ToxMod. https://www.modulate.ai/toxmod/gaming/. Accessed 1 Sept 2024
17. Harreld, J.B., O'Reilly, C.A., III., Tushman, M.L.: Dynamic capabilities at IBM: driving strategy into action. Calif. Manage. Rev. **49**(4), 21–43 (2007)
18. Descript: Overdub. https://www.descript.com/overdub/. Accessed 1 Sept 2024
19. iSpeech: iSpeech. https://www.ispeech.org/. Accessed 1 Sept 2024
20. Resemble AI: Resemble AI. https://www.resemble.ai/. Accessed 1 Sept 2024
21. Zhang, L.-J., Shan, Z., Mao, Z.-H.: An optimal-control-based decision-making model and consulting methodology for service enterprises. IEEE Trans. Eng. Manage. **57**(4), 607–619 (2010). https://doi.org/10.1109/TEM.2009.2034270

Exploring Experiential Marketing Strategies of Luxury Fashion Brands in the Metaverse: An In-Depth Analysis of Immersive Consumer Engagement

Wang Yang[1], Fusheng Tan[2](✉), Yuqi Bai[1], and Jee-hun Ryu[3]

[1] Tarim University, Xinjiang Production and Construction Corps, Alaer City, China
[2] Ordos Research Institute of Liaoning Technical University, Ordos, China
740467420@qq.com
[3] 50 Gamasil-ro, Hayang-Eup, Gyeongsan-Si, Gyeongsangbuk-Do, Republic of Korea

Abstract. The Metaverse, integrating Virtual Reality (VR), Augmented Reality (AR), and digital twin technologies, has emerged as a transformative platform offering new opportunities for luxury fashion brands. This study explores how these brands can leverage experiential marketing in the Metaverse to enhance brand value and market competitiveness. By aligning with the Metaverse's immersive and interactive nature, luxury brands can extend their traditional focus on personalized customer experiences. This research identifies key experiential marketing elements—such as virtual try-ons, interactive advertising, and brand storytelling—as foundations for effective strategies. Using both qualitative and quantitative methods, including in-depth interviews and surveys, the study examines the relationships between perceived experiential value, satisfaction, brand identification, and purchase intentions. The findings demonstrate that immersive experiences and high interactivity within the Metaverse significantly boost consumers' perceived value of luxury brands, increasing satisfaction and brand loyalty, and driving purchasing behavior. This study offers valuable insights for luxury brands on crafting effective experiential marketing strategies in the Metaverse, providing a competitive edge in an increasingly digital market.

Keywords: Metaverse · Luxury Fashion Brands · Experiential Marketing

1 Introduction

The Metaverse, originally conceptualized in Neal Stephenson's 1992 novel "Snow Crash," has transitioned from fiction to reality, fueled by advancements in VR, AR, 5G, and AI technologies. The global push towards digital transformation, accelerated by the COVID-19 pandemic, has positioned the Metaverse as a critical platform for innovation across industries. For luxury fashion brands, renowned for offering personalized experiences, the Metaverse presents a unique opportunity to deepen customer loyalty and enhance brand value through immersive and interactive experiences.

This work was supported by the Chinese Ministry of Education Humanities and Social Sciences Research Project "Research on Digital Conservation of Typical Traditional Costumes of Minority Ethnic Groups in Xinjiang" Project No. 23XJJC760001.

S. He and L.-J. Zhang (Eds.): SCF/SCC 2024, LNCS 15430, pp. 100–113, 2025.
https://doi.org/10.1007/978-3-031-77000-5_7

Experiential marketing, which has evolved to leverage advanced digital technologies, plays a pivotal role in this context. Pine and Gilmore's (1998) experience economy theory emphasized the shift from products to experiences as key market differentiators. Schmitt (1999) expanded on this by identifying five experiential dimensions—sensory, emotional, cognitive, behavioral, and relational—that connect brands with consumers on a deeper level.

In the Metaverse, these experiential elements are further amplified, allowing brands to simulate real-world interactions in a virtual environment. This paper explores how luxury fashion brands can utilize the Metaverse to enhance experiential marketing strategies, ultimately influencing consumer behavior and brand perception.

Using a mixed-methods approach, this study combines qualitative insights from consumer interviews with quantitative data from surveys to analyze the effectiveness of these strategies. The findings highlight the Metaverse's potential as a powerful tool for luxury brands to create deeply resonant, immersive experiences.

2 Metaverse, Luxury Goods and Experiential Marketing Theory

2.1 The Concept of the Metaverse

The term "Metaverse" first appeared in Neal Stephenson's science fiction novel, where it was used to describe a successor to the internet based on virtual reality [1]. The word "Metaverse" is a combination of "Meta" (meaning "beyond") and "Universe," signifying a new virtual universe created beyond the physical world. Thus, the Metaverse is a 3D virtual world with enhanced social significance [2], offering users limitless opportunities for social interaction [3]. Four key elements define the Metaverse: Augmented Reality (AR), Lifelogging, Mirror World, and Virtual Reality (VR).

2.2 Luxury Fashion Brand Concept

In English dictionaries, "luxury" and "luxus" are considered synonyms. The term "luxus" originates from Latin, meaning "luxury, excess" [4]. Tracing its etymology, the word derives from ancient European languages, encompassing meanings such as "twist," "abundance," and "disorder due to displacement". Today, the concept of luxury goods refers to consumer products that exceed the basic needs for survival and development, characterized by uniqueness, scarcity, and high value—often considered non-essential items. Over time, the concept of luxury has evolved. Modern luxury is not only a symbol of wealth but also an expression of personal taste, uniqueness, and craftsmanship [5]. The researcher in this study defines luxury goods as unique, scarce, and exceptional consumer products that exceed the basic needs for human survival and development. While most scholars view luxury goods as symbols of waste and extravagance, some consider them products that promote economic development.

2.3 Luxury Fashion Brand Marketing

The financial crisis in 2009 led many luxury brands to adopt digital marketing, helping maintain brand visibility despite economic challenges. Early digital initiatives, like

Burberry's "Art of the Trench," marked the beginning of luxury e-commerce. Since the onset of the COVID-19 pandemic, especially from 2019 onwards, luxury brands' marketing strategies have undergone significant changes. The year 2020 is seen as the inaugural year of the Metaverse, symbolizing the advent of a new era in digital marketing. Research shows that post-pandemic, over 66% of consumers across different age groups and regions visit a brand's e-commerce site before making in-store purchases [6]. Leading gaming platforms include Roblox, Minecraft, and Fortnite, with Roblox boasting over 200 million monthly active users. Another popular construction game, Minecraft, has nearly 180 million active users, while Fortnite has 70 million active users. Luxury brands such as Louis Vuitton, Gucci, Burberry, and Balenciaga have associated with these platforms. Metaverse marketing is anticipated to be the future direction of marketing [7].

2.4 Experiential Marketing's Role in Metaverse Marketing

Experiential marketing focuses on creating memorable consumer experiences, moving beyond product sales to emotional and sensory engagement. B. Joseph Pine II and James H. Gilmore first introduced this concept in 1998, noting that traditional marketing methods no longer satisfy the needs of modern consumers who seek not only material fulfillment but also emotional and sensory appeal. Subsequently, in 1999, Schmitt further developed this concept in his book *Experiential Marketing: How to Build Brands in the Minds of Consumers*, where he emphasized five types of experiences: sensory experiences (Sense), emotional experiences (Feel), cognitive experiences (Think), behavioral experiences (Act), and relational experiences (Relate) [8] (see Fig. 1).

In the Metaverse, these experiences are enhanced by the immersive nature of digital environments, allowing brands to create fully integrated and unforgettable consumer interactions.

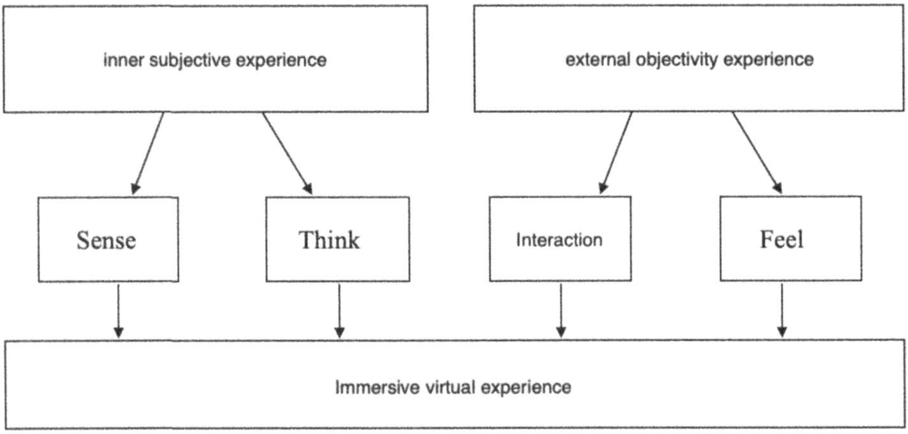

Fig. 1. Four Dimensions of Immersive Experience

3 Research Design

3.1 Research Model

This study develops a research model based on literature and case analysis, confirming that experiential elements in the Metaverse significantly influence user immersion, satisfaction, and repurchase intention. The model examines how different types of marketing within the Metaverse interact with experiential elements and how these interactions shape consumer attitudes.

To further understand the impact of brand perceptions on satisfaction and the variability of immersion across age groups, additional experimental studies are proposed. These studies aim to explore the full potential of brand experiential marketing within the Metaverse and its integration into current and future strategies.

The research model, depicted in [see Fig. 2], guides the empirical research to validate the proposed brand experiential marketing framework.

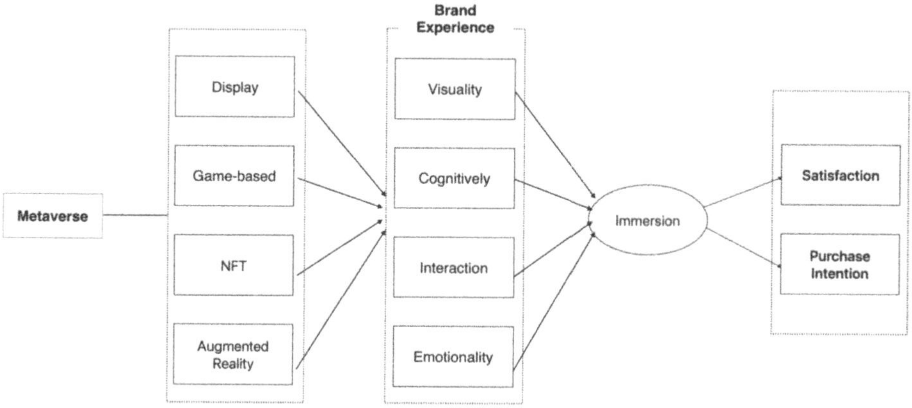

Fig. 2. Model Validation through Exploration of Significant Relationships

This study validates the research model by examining the significant relationships between Metaverse types, experiential elements, immersion, satisfaction, and repurchase intention. The model, based on a user experience framework, consists of seven variables, with connections represented by paths.

The independent variables—experiential elements (sensory, cognitive, emotional, interactive)—are linked to the dependent variable, immersion. Previous studies have highlighted the importance of immersion in the Metaverse, expanding from technological aspects to consumer experiences. For example, research by Kim Chaeyoon and Kwon Ji-eun found that synchronized visual and auditory elements enhance audience immersion and interaction. Similarly, studies by Lee Hye-won and others suggest that aesthetic and interactive elements within the Metaverse can significantly impact user immersion and overall brand perception.

This study hypothesizes that system-based experiential elements influence consumer immersion, which in turn affects satisfaction and repurchase intention. Satisfaction itself is hypothesized to influence repurchase intention. Previous models, such as the Chinese Customer Satisfaction Index (CCSI), adapted from the American Customer Satisfaction Index (ACSI), inform this research's approach to quality assessment.

The proposed model explores these relationships across four Metaverse types (Exhibition-based, Game-based, NFT-based, XR-based) and is validated through empirical research without distinguishing between variables in each context.

3.2 Hypothesis Development

Based on the research model, hypotheses were developed and tested to validate the experiential marketing framework. These hypotheses focus on the significant relationships between the identified variables, with each research model examining the interactions between independent and dependent variables (see Fig. 3).

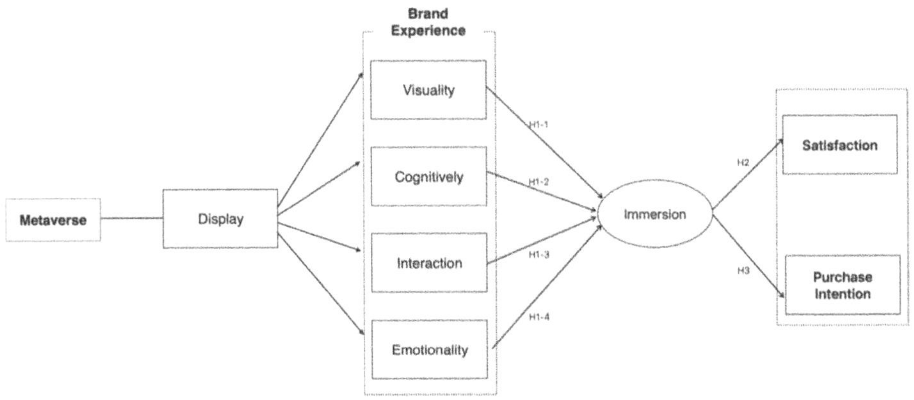

Fig. 3. Empirical Research Model for Exhibition-Based Metaverse Marketing

The model is designed to examine the relationships between brand experiential elements, immersion, satisfaction, and repurchase intention within the context of the exhibition-type Metaverse. Additionally, it considers age as a moderating variable to study the impact of sensory and cognitive elements on immersion. Research has shown that consumers sharing brand stories have a positive impact on brand story recognition and consumer attitudes [9]. Brand story recognition is a critical component of brand equity, positively influencing brand awareness, brand image, and purchase intention. The core hypotheses are grounded in specific consumer behaviors and market trends [10], which help provide deeper and more accurate analyses of the effectiveness of marketing strategies. Thus, these hypotheses explore how specific types of marketing can have unique impacts across different consumer groups, revealing more detailed market insights and strategic guidance. The research model is illustrated in Fig. 2-2-1, and the research hypotheses are as follows:

- H1-1: The sensory elements in exhibition-type Metaverse marketing have a positive impact on immersion.

- H1-2: The cognitive elements in exhibition-type Metaverse marketing have a positive impact on immersion.
- H1-3: The interactive elements in exhibition-type Metaverse marketing have a positive impact on immersion.
- H1-4: The emotional elements in exhibition-type Metaverse marketing have a negative impact on immersion.
- H2: The immersion elements in exhibition-type Metaverse marketing have a positive impact on satisfaction.
- H3: The immersion elements in exhibition-type Metaverse marketing have a positive impact on repurchase intention.

3.3 Data Collection and Analysis

This study aims to validate the influence of luxury brand experiential elements on repurchase intention through the mediating effect of satisfaction, driven by immersion, from a Metaverse perspective. The data was collected from individuals with online shopping experience, considering various demographic variables, and the sample was structured to reflect a balanced demographic distribution.

The survey was conducted over a period of 28 days, from January 11 to February 7, 2024. Both online and offline questionnaires were administered to 510 general consumers with experience in purchasing luxury goods. To ensure the quality of the survey, responses that were deemed careless or incomplete were excluded (All answers are the same or incomplete.). Ultimately, data from 489 valid questionnaires completed by consumers with luxury purchasing experience were used for empirical analysis.

To validate the research hypotheses, this study employed SPSS 26.0 and AMOS 24.0 statistical software for technical statistical analysis of the collected questionnaires. In accordance with the research procedure, the following specific statistical analysis methods were applied:

Frequency Analysis: To understand the demographic characteristics of the research subjects, a frequency analysis was conducted.

Exploratory Analysis, Reliability Analysis, Confirmatory Factor Analysis, and Correlation Analysis: These analyses were performed to confirm the applicability and accuracy of the structural concepts of experiential marketing in luxury brand marketing from a Metaverse perspective. The four dimensions analyzed were sensory, emotional, cognitive, and interactive elements.

Structural Equation Modeling (SEM) and Path Analysis: To verify the relationships between experiential elements and immersion, as well as the relationships between immersion and consumer behavior, SEM and path analysis were conducted.

Regression Analysis: Finally, to validate the mediating effects of experiential elements, regression analysis was performed.

These analyses provided a comprehensive understanding of how experiential elements influence immersion, satisfaction, and repurchase intention within the Metaverse environment, supporting the verification of the proposed research hypotheses.

4 Demographic Characteristics

In this study, to understand the demographic characteristics of the survey respondents, a frequency analysis was conducted on five key variables: gender, age, occupation, education level, and monthly income.

Frequency Analysis: First, a frequency analysis was performed to provide an overview of the demographic characteristics of the research subjects.

Validity, Reliability, Confirmatory Factor Analysis, and Correlation Analysis: Next, to validate the applicability and accuracy of the structural concepts of experiential marketing—specifically sensory, emotional, cognitive, and interactive elements—in luxury brand marketing within the Metaverse context, several analyses were conducted. These included validity analysis, reliability analysis, confirmatory factor analysis (CFA), and correlation analysis.

Structural Equation Modeling (SEM) and Path Analysis: To verify the relationships between experiential elements and immersion, as well as the relationships between immersion and consumer behavior, SEM and path analysis were performed.

Regression Analysis: Finally, to examine the mediating effects of experiential elements, regression analysis was conducted.

These analyses provided insights into how demographic factors influence the study variables and how experiential marketing elements impact immersion, satisfaction, and repurchase intentions within the Metaverse environment.

4.1 Reliability and Validity Analysis

Reliability Verification: Reliability analysis is used to measure the consistency and stability of the questionnaire data. It is primarily employed to determine whether the data collected through the questionnaire is reliable and stable. This is typically assessed using the Cronbach's Alpha (α) value, which is widely recognized in the academic community for evaluating the reliability of a questionnaire. The Cronbach's Alpha coefficients of individual variables and the overall variables are used to judge the internal consistency of the variables. When the Cronbach's Alpha coefficient for both individual variables and the overall variables is greater than 0.7, the variable is considered reliable and to have internal consistency [11].

In this study, the Corrected Item-Total Correlation (CITC) values for all items in the exhibition-type model were greater than 0.4, indicating that no item would significantly increase reliability if deleted. Therefore, all items are valuable and should be retained. The internal consistency coefficient for this scale was 0.820, and the reliability indicators for all variables were greater than 0.8. This suggests that the results are highly stable, and the scale demonstrates very good reliability.

4.2 Confirmatory Factor Analysis

The validity evaluation of the exhibition-type scale includes both content validity and construct validity. The evaluation metrics chosen in this study are based on scales validated domestically and internationally, which were developed after multiple reviews by relevant experts and professors. The results of the exploratory factor analysis were also quite favorable, indicating good content validity. Construct validity can be assessed through Confirmatory Factor Analysis (CFA), which includes both convergent validity and discriminant validity. The indicators used to evaluate convergent validity include factor loadings, Composite Reliability (CR), and Average Variance Extracted (AVE).

In this study, CFA was conducted using AMOS 24.0 software, taking measurement errors into account for the scales and other measurement tools. For CFA, each item's factor loading should exceed 0.6, and the model's fit indices must meet the corresponding standards. The primary fit indices include the Chi-square value, degrees of freedom, Chi-square/degrees of freedom ratio, RMSEA (Root Mean Square Error of Approximation), IFI (Incremental Fit Index), TLI (Tucker-Lewis Index), and CFI (Comparative Fit Index). When all these indices simultaneously meet the standards, the model's fit is considered to be good. The Composite Reliability (CR) and Average Variance Extracted (AVE) are calculated based on the standardized factor loadings. When CR exceeds 0.7 and AVE exceeds 0.5, the measurement variables are considered to have good convergent validity [12].

The analysis results indicated that all fit indices for the model were within reasonable ranges and met the required standards. Therefore, the model demonstrates good fit and is suitable for further validation.

4.3 Correlation Analysis

Correlation analysis is used to examine the relationship between variables to determine whether they are related and the strength of their relationship. The significance coefficient is used to confirm whether a significant relationship exists between two variables, while the correlation coefficient indicates whether the relationship is positive or negative, as well as the degree of closeness between the variables. Common correlation coefficients include Pearson, Spearman, and Kendall correlation coefficients. In this study, considering the characteristics of the sample data and methods used by other researchers, Pearson correlation coefficients were employed to verify the correlations between the model variables.

Exhibition-Type Correlation Analysis.

As shown in Tables 1, 2, 3 and 4, the correlation coefficient between sensory experience and immersion is 0.458, indicating a positive correlation between the two. Thus, the positive relationship between sensory experience and immersion is preliminarily validated. Similarly, the correlations between cognitive experience, interactive experience, emotional experience, satisfaction, repurchase intention, and immersion have also been confirmed.

This analysis suggests that various experiential elements (sensory, cognitive, interactive, and emotional) are significantly related to immersion, and these relationships can influence satisfaction and repurchase intentions in the context of exhibition-type Metaverse marketing.

4.4 Hypothesis Testing for Exhibition-Type Experience

To verify the impact of experiential dimensions on immersion, a regression analysis was conducted, focusing on the effects of emotional experience, sensory experience, cognitive experience, and interactive experience on immersion. According to the results in the table, the Variance Inflation Factor (VIF) values for the variables in the model are 1.096, 1.195, 1.257, and 1.111, respectively. All VIF values are less than 5, indicating that there is no multicollinearity issue among the independent variables in the regression equation, meaning the model is free from multicollinearity problems. The Durbin-Watson (D-W) value of the model is 1.996, which is close to 2, suggesting that there is no autocorrelation problem in the model, and the model structure is sound.

Next, the regression results of the model were analyzed. The R-squared value of the model is 0.432, indicating a good fit for the model. Additionally, the model passed the F-test ($F = 51.426$, $p = 0.000 < 0.001$), further proving the model's validity and applicability (see Fig. 4).

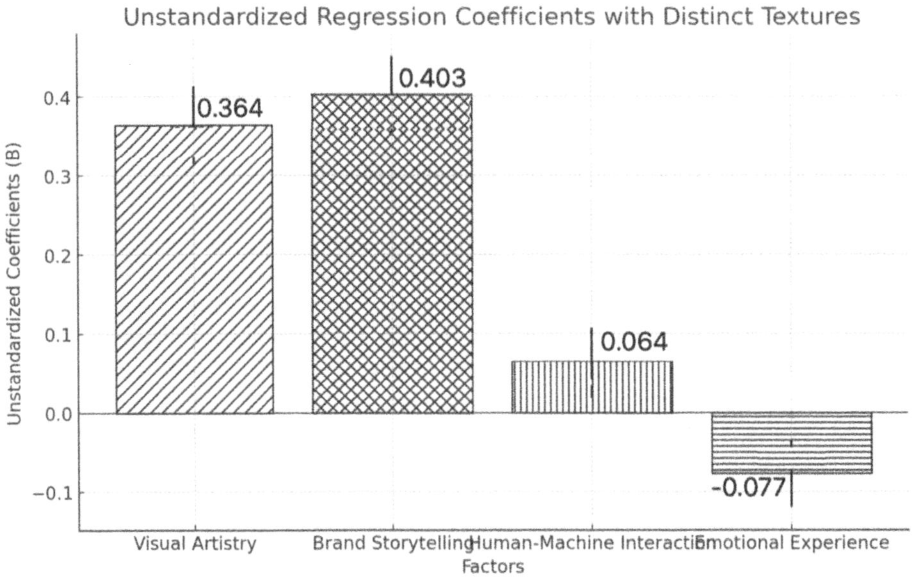

Fig. 4. The regression analysis results indicate the following:

Sensory Experience: The sensory experience has a positive and significant impact on immersion ($Beta = 0.360$, $p < 0.001$), confirming that sensory elements contribute positively to user immersion in the exhibition-type Metaverse.

Cognitive Experience: Cognitive experience also has a positive and significant impact on immersion (Beta = 0.418, $p < 0.001$), suggesting that cognitive elements strongly influence immersion.

Interactive Experience: Interactive experience has a positive but not statistically significant impact on immersion (Beta = 0.076, p = 0.143), indicating that while there may be a positive relationship, it is not strong enough to be considered significant in this model.

Emotional Experience: Emotional experience shows a negative impact on immersion (Beta = −0.086), but this relationship is not statistically significant (p = 0.076), implying that the emotional aspect might have a varying effect on immersion depending on other factors.

These findings support the hypotheses related to sensory and cognitive experiences' positive effects on immersion but do not fully support the hypotheses regarding interactive and emotional experiences within the exhibition-type Metaverse marketing context.

[Fig. 3] Non-Standardized Regression Coefficients.

H1-1 Hypothesis: It was hypothesized that sensory elements in the exhibition type would positively influence immersion. The regression analysis results showed that the coefficient for this factor is positive (0.364), with a p-value less than 0.05, indicating a significant positive effect of sensory elements on immersion. Therefore, the H1-1 hypothesis is supported.

H1-2 Hypothesis: It was hypothesized that cognitive elements in the exhibition type would positively influence immersion. The statistical analysis results showed that the coefficient for this factor is positive (0.403), with a very low p-value, indicating a significant positive impact of cognitive elements on immersion. Therefore, the H1-2 hypothesis is also supported.

H1-3 Hypothesis: It was hypothesized that interactive elements in the exhibition type would positively influence immersion. However, despite the positive coefficient for this factor (0.064), the p-value is 0.143, which does not reach the level of statistical significance. Therefore, the H1-3 hypothesis is not supported.

H1-4 Hypothesis: It was hypothesized that emotional elements in the exhibition type would negatively influence immersion. Although the coefficient for this factor is negative (-0.077), the p-value is 0.076, which is not statistically significant. Therefore, the H1-4 hypothesis is also not supported.

Regression Analysis on the Impact of Immersion on Consumer Satisfaction and Repurchase Intention.

To verify the impact of immersion on consumer satisfaction and repurchase intention, regression analyses were conducted.

Model for Satisfaction as the Dependent Variable: The Durbin-Watson (D-W) value of the model is 2.092, close to 2, indicating no autocorrelation issue and good model structure. The R-squared value of the model is 0.025, and it passed the F-test (F = 7.117, $p = 0.008 < 0.01$), indicating the model's validity.

Model for Repurchase Intention as the Dependent Variable: The D-W value of this model is 1.815, also close to 2, indicating no autocorrelation problem and a well-structured model. However, the R-squared value is only 0.006, and it did not pass the

F-test ($F = 1.686$, $p > 0.05$), indicating insufficient explanatory power for repurchase intention.

H2 Hypothesis: It was hypothesized that immersive factors in the exhibition type would positively influence satisfaction. The analysis results showed that the coefficient for the immersive factor is 0.184, with a t-value of 2.668 and a p-value of 0.008. These results are statistically significant, supporting the H2 hypothesis that immersion positively affects satisfaction.

H3 Hypothesis: It was hypothesized that immersive factors in the exhibition type would also positively influence repurchase intention. However, the analysis results showed that the coefficient for the immersive factor is 0.090, with a t-value of 1.298 and a p-value of 0.195, which did not reach statistical significance. Therefore, the H3 hypothesis that immersion significantly affects repurchase intention is not supported.

Sensory and cognitive experiences within exhibition-type interactions in the Metaverse have a significant positive impact on immersion, while interactive and emotional experiences do not show a significant effect. This suggests that in the Metaverse environment, sensory and cognitive factors play a crucial role in enhancing consumer immersion. Exhibition-type experiential marketing in the Metaverse not only allows for the highly customized virtual display of products but also conveys richer and more engaging brand stories.

This marketing strategy opens up a new stage for luxury fashion brands, extending beyond mere product display to creating novel interactive brand experiences. Such a strategy is vital for modern luxury brands in shaping brand image and maintaining customer relationships. By leveraging the immersive capabilities of the Metaverse, brands can craft experiences that resonate deeply with consumers, fostering stronger emotional connections and reinforcing brand loyalty. This approach is essential for luxury brands aiming to remain competitive and relevant in the rapidly evolving digital landscape.

5 Conclusion

In recent years, the advent of artificial intelligence technologies like OpenAI's ChatGPT has captured widespread attention, momentarily overshadowing the buzz around the Metaverse. However, continuous technological advancements have not only reduced design costs but also enhanced the capabilities of head-mounted displays and VR glasses. These developments have provided brands with innovative content marketing platforms, prompting an increasing number to venture into Metaverse marketing.

Given that Metaverse marketing remains relatively novel and complex for most consumers in the Chinese market, this study offers pivotal insights for brands and marketing agencies formulating strategies in this domain. Exhibition-type marketing, in particular, emphasizes immersive brand storytelling and product showcases, effectively virtualizing real-world brand exhibitions or museums. Leveraging cutting-edge 3D technologies and exhibition methods, this approach delivers vibrant visuals and prominent brand imagery. It seamlessly integrates music to facilitate explorations within immersive virtual spaces, enhancing emotional resonance and fashion choices through tailored digital experiences.

Brands can create virtual museums to exhibit their history and flagship products, employing storytelling and immersive interactions to deepen consumer understanding and emotional engagement with the brand culture. High-resolution images and 360-degree video technologies can showcase product intricacies, while interactive learning modules delve into the historical backgrounds of brand founders, design philosophies, and major achievements. Post-exhibition, users can engage in online discussions to share their perspectives and vote on themes for future exhibitions. Incorporating interactive brand stories allows users to navigate different chapters of the brand's history through varied storylines. Additionally, integrating AI-guided NPCs within virtual museums can offer real-time, customized tours based on user interests and interactions.

The Metaverse, as an emerging digital frontier, presents unprecedented opportunities for brand marketing. As technology continues to evolve, brands must innovate their marketing strategies to adapt to the rapidly changing digital landscape. By effectively harnessing the four experiential elements—sensory, cognitive, interactive, and emotional—brands can cultivate profound consumer immersion within the Metaverse, distinguishing themselves in a fiercely competitive market.

Looking ahead, brands should prioritize personalized and customized experiences to cater to the increasingly diverse consumer demands. The Metaverse transcends being merely a platform for brand image display; it serves as a bridge for establishing deep-seated connections with consumers. Brands must seize this opportunity, melding innovation with technology, to craft forward-thinking marketing strategies that ensure enduring success in the digital age.

Appendix

Table 1. Criteria for Fit Indices

Fit Index	Critical Value	Current Value	Result
Chi-square	-	500.952	-
Degrees of Freedom	-	413	-
$\chi 2$ /df	<3	1.213	Applicable
Root Mean Square Error (RMSEA)	<0.10	0.028	Applicable
Normed Fit Index (NFI)	>0.9	0.906	Applicable
Incremental Fit Index (IFI)	>0.9	0.982	Applicable
Tucker-Lewis Index (TLI)	>0.9	0.980	Applicable
Comparative Fit Index (CFI)	> 0.9	0.982	Applicable

Table 2. Correlation Analysis Results

Item	Sensory	Cognitive	Interactive	Emotional	Immersive	Satisfaction	Repurchase Intention
Sensory	1						
Cognitive	0.167	1					
Interactive	0.288	0.355	1				
Emotional	−0.081	−0.265	−0.254	1			
Immersive	0.458	0.527	0.349	−0.245	1		
Satisfaction	0.098	−0.009	0.017	−0.013	0.159	1	
Repurchase Intention	0.028	−0.021	−0.047	−0.033	0.078	0.086	1

* Significance levels: $p < 0.05$, p < 0.01, * p < 0.001.

Table 3. Regression Analysis of the Impact of Brand Exhibition Experience Dimensions on Immersion

Exhibition-Type	Unstandardized Coefficients	Standardized Coefficients	t-value	Significance	Collinearity Statistics
	B	Standard Error	Beta		Tolerance
(Constant)	0.865	0.251		3.444	0.001
Sensory	0.364	0.049	0.360	7.492	0.000
Cognitive	0.403	0.048	0.418	8.333	0.000
Interactive	0.064	0.043	0.076	1.469	0.143
Emotional	−0.077	0.043	−0.086	−1.779	0.076

Table 4. Regression Analysis of the Impact of Experience Dimensions on Immersion in Exhibition Type

Dependent Variable	Unstandardized Coefficients	Standardized Coefficients	t-value	Significance
	B	Standard Error	Beta	
Satisfaction				
(Constant)	2.442	0.225		10.870
Immersive	0.184	0.069	0.159	2.668
Repurchase Intention				
(Constant)	2.728	0.225		12.108
Immersive	0.090	0.069	0.078	1.298

References

1. Stephenson, N.: Snow Crash. Penguin Books Australia (2011)
2. Joshua, J.: Information bodies: computational anxiety in Neal Stephensons snow crash. Interdisc. Literary Stud. **19**(1), 17–47 (2017)
3. Dionisio, J.D.N., Iii, W.G.B., Gilbert, R.: 3D virtual worlds and the metaverse: current status and future possibilities. ACM Comput. Surv. (CSUR) **45**(3), 1–38 (2013)
4. Calefato, P.: Luxury: Fashion, Lifestyles, and Excess, pp. 9–10. Bloomsbury, New York (1988)
5. Kapferer, J.N., Bastien, V.: The specificity of luxury management: turning marketing upside down. In: Kapferer, JN., Kernstock, J., Brexendorf, T., Powell, S. (eds.) Advances in Luxury Brand Management, pp. 65–84. Palgrave Macmillan, Cham (2017). https://doi.org/10.1007/978-3-319-51127-6_5
6. Bain & Company: Bain & Company & the Comité Colbert find accelerated adoption of sophisticated technologies in the luxury sector. Bain & Company (2023)
7. Dwivedi, Y.K., et al.: Metaverse marketing: how the metaverse will shape the future of consumer research and practice. Psychol. Mark. **40**(4), 750–776 (2023)
8. Schmitt, B.: Experiential marketing. J. Mark. Manag. **15**(1–3), 53–67 (1999)
9. Hong, J., Yang, J., Wooldridge, B.R., Bhappu, A.D.: Sharing consumers' brand storytelling: influence of consumers' storytelling on brand attitude via emotions and cognitions. J. Product Brand Manag. **31**(2), 265–278 (2022)
10. Yoo, S.C.: Brand Story that Works: Creating Branded Stories in the Era of Social Content (2020)
11. Bland, J.M., Altman, D.G.: Statistics notes: Cronbach's alpha. BMJ **314**(7080), 572 (1997)
12. Hair, J.F.: Multivariate Data Analysis (2009)

Author Index

S. He and L.-J. Zhang (Eds.): SCF/SCC 2024, LNCS 15430, p. 115, 2025.
https://doi.org/10.1007/978-3-031-77000-5

SPRINGER NATURE

GPSR Compliance

The European Union's (EU) General Product Safety Regulation (GPSR) is a set of rules that requires consumer products to be safe and our obligations to ensure this.

If you have any concerns about our products, you can contact us on ProductSafety@springernature.com

In case Publisher is established outside the EU, the EU authorized representative is:

Springer Nature Customer Service Center GmbH
Europaplatz 3
69115 Heidelberg, Germany

The manufacturer's authorised representative in the EU is Springer Nature Customer Service Centre GmbH, Europaplatz 3, 69115 Heidelberg, Germany. If you have any concerns regarding our products, please contact ProductSafety@springernature.com

Printed and bound by CPI Group (UK) Ltd, Croydon, CR0 4YY
01/10/2026
02225843-0003